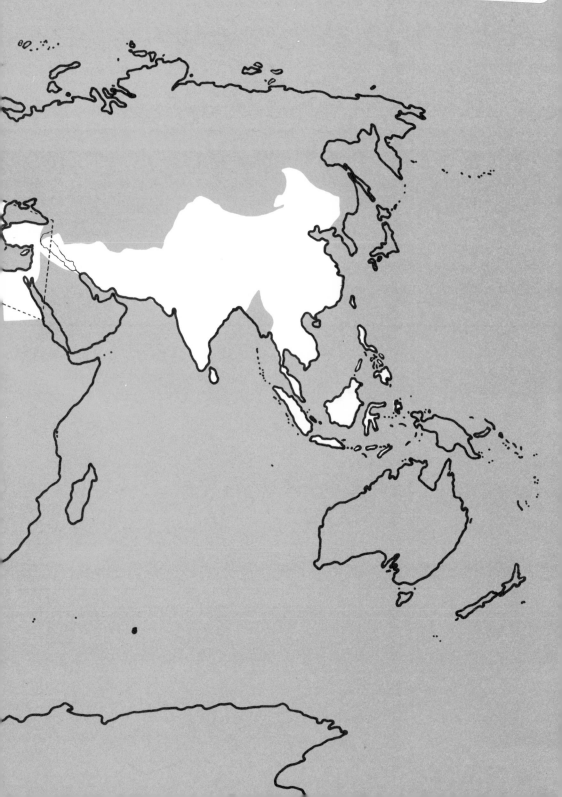

MESOPOTAMIA	Jean-Claude Margueron, Agrégé of the University; Member of the French Institute of Archaeology of Beirut
MEXICO	Jacques Soustelle
PERSIA I (From the origins to the Achaemenids)	Jean-Louis Huot, Agrégé of the University; Member of the French Institute of Archaeology of Beirut
PERSIA II (From the Seleucids to the Sassanids)	Vladimir Lukonin, Curator at the Hermitage Museum, Leningrad
PERU	Rafael Larco Hoyle †, Director of the Rafael Larco Herrera Museum, Lima
PREHISTORY	Denise de Sonneville-Bordes, Ph. D.
SOUTHERN CAUCASUS	Boris B. Piotrovsky, Director of the Hermitage Museum, Leningrad
SOUTHERN SIBERIA	Mikhail Gryaznov, Professor at the Archaeological Institute of Leningrad
SYRIA-PALESTINE I (Ancient Orient)	Jean Perrot, Head of the French Archaeological Mission in Israel
SYRIA-PALESTINE II (Classical Orient)	Michael Avi Yonah, Professor at the Hebrew University of Jerusalem
THE TEUTONS	R. Hachmann, Professor at the University of Saarbrücken
URARTU	Boris B. Piotrovsky, Director of the Hermitage Museum, Leningrad

ANCIENT CIVILIZATIONS

Series prepared under the direction of
Jean Marcadé, Professor of Archaeology
at the University of Bordeaux

THE ANCIENT CIVILIZATION OF

ROME

GILBERT *charles-* PICARD

Translated from the French by H.S.B. HARRISON

62 illustrations in colour; 130 illustrations in black and white

COWLES BOOK COMPANY, INC.
488 MADISON AVENUE
NEW YORK, N.Y. 10022

CONTENTS

PREFACE

Archaeology has many aspects, and the Ancient Civilizations *series aims at presenting them all. Taking each sector of this vast field in turn, it analyses the conditions and spirit in which it is being explored, the special problems connected with it, the methods used, and the results achieved. Thus, as the series grows, an overall picture will emerge of archaeology as it is today. Though still a young science, it has ceased to be a dilettante's pastime. No longer simply a means of filling museums with attractive exhibits and providing material for the history of art, it has become the handmaid of history itself. There are even periods — in fact, whole civilizations—for which, in the absence of written or decipherable sources, archaeology replaces history.*

This is not, of course, the case with ancient Rome, which has left a vast literature. Nevertheless, archaeology is of inestimable help in checking, correcting, or completing what the Latin authors—even the annalists and historians— have written about the early days of Rome, which were already lost in the mists of legend when they dealt with them. The first concrete details on everyday life in the ancient world came from the excavations at Herculaneum and Pompeii. By means of archaeological investigations and the statistical interpretation of the results, increasing light is being thrown on such questions as town planning and administration, supplies of raw materials, and trade. Finally, even more than the literature, the imagery of the frescoes and sculptures reveals the forms taken by Roman cultural influence in the outposts of the Empire, religious trends in the far-off provinces and in Rome itself, and the spiritual and moral aspirations of people of all classes.

Such findings add a new dimension—or at least a deeper human interest—to history.

J.M.

9

We should like to express our sincere gratitude to all those who kindly helped us compile this work. We are particularly grateful to the following Museums for their generosity in supplying us with material: the Palazzo dei Conservatori and Capitoline Museums in Rome, the Musée d'art et d'histoire in Geneva, the Musée Romain at Avenches and the Bardo Museum in Tunis.

We must also thank Dr. Luciano Merlo of Rome for the valuable and devoted assistance he so readily gave us while this book was in preparation.

THE HISTORY
OF ROMAN ARCHAEOLOGY

I

The beginnings: Herculaneum and Pompeii (Plates 1-10)

Archaeological studies might never have developed if two small towns of the Campania—Herculaneum and Pompeii—had not been engulfed, in the space of a few hours, by an eruption of Vesuvius on 23-24 August A.D. 79. Though we might like to believe otherwise, dying in one's bed at the end of a peaceful life is not the best means of going down to posterity. When life continues in the same place, when the same field is tilled for centuries, when the son succeeds the father from generation to generation in a settled community, the vestiges of the past are wiped out far more thoroughly than by the onslaughts of man or nature. The situation is quite different, however, when an overwhelming disaster causes life to stop, but covers the remains with a protective "wrapping". This is precisely what happened at Herculaneum and Pompeii: the first was swallowed up in volcanic mud which subsequently hardened into a kind of tufa; a shower of ashes and pebbles buried the second under a shroud several yards thick. The dead cities were thus protected from plunderers. Graffiti testify to a few attempts to explore them in ancient times; in the Middle Ages and for long afterwards their existence was practically forgotten.

The excavations started at Herculaneum by the Prince d'Elbeuf in 1719 mark the beginning of a new era. It is true that this Austrian nobleman—like others who had investigated ancient monuments before him, from the Renaissance onwards—was primarily interested in enriching his collection of precious objects, rather than in providing historians with new data that would help them reconstruct Roman civilization. Although his excavations of the buried cities were carried out in a way that now strikes us as crude, if not barbarous, and much valuable evidence was utterly destroyed, they nevertheless showed for the first time that in some cases the background to the life of the past had survived intact.

It is true that, before this discovery, a great number of classical buildings, most of them Roman, had been carefully studied. But these—though often admirably preserved—were divorced from their original settings. At Herculaneum and Pompeii, however, a substantial fragment of the ancient world had survived unchanged. Its re-emergence made a profound impression, and altered the whole aesthetic outlook of the period.

It was certainly fortunate that the civilisation concerned was that of ancient Rome, about which 18th-century Europeans already knew a great deal. From their earliest years they had been nurtured in the spiritual heritage of the Romans, and the writings of Cicero, Virgil, Horace, and Plutarch—who, though Greek, was Roman in spirit—were more familiar to them than many works only a few generations old. Many of their ideas about the classical world were inaccurate, however, as archaeology and the other "auxiliary sciences" of history would prove: Montesquieu, for instance, completely misunderstood the Romans. The 18th century was chiefly interested in the early days of Rome and the beginnings of the Republic—the era of that *virtus* which the French revolutionaries took as their ideal. The ruins brought to light belonged, however, to the Imperial era, and people took a long time to realize that Roman civilization had undergone profound changes between the ages of Romulus and Cincinnatus and that of the Empire. For example, L. David naively copied the costumes and arms of his "Horaces" from Trajan's Column, without apparently realizing that fashions must have changed somewhat over a period of eight centuries.

The Villa of the Papyri

Probably the most noteworthy of these 18th-century discoveries was made at Herculaneum in 1750 by the Swiss architect, Charles Weber, working for Charles of Bourbon. This was a suburban villa, half-way up a spur of Vesuvius, with terraced gardens stretching down to the sea. The architect had reduced the traditional features of the Roman villa—the *atrium* and its dependencies—to the role of a simple entrance, giving greater emphasis to the courtyards and colonnaded gardens. These constitued an open-air museum, containing excellent replicas of Greek works: a seated Hermes, after Lysippus; the "Dancing Women" wearing the severe Doric peplum; and the two sleeping Satyrs that are now the pride of the Department of Bronzes in the Museum of Naples. There was also a whole gallery of men of letters. The owner was obviously an intellectual, and his library was full of scrolls of papyri, which could still be deciphered even though they were partially charred. They included the works of Philodemus, a philosopher of the Epicurean school, who lived in the 1st century B.C. and, according to Cicero, enjoyed the protection of L. Calpurnius Piso, Julius Caesar's father-in-law. From this, an Italian scholar, Comparetti, has concluded that the Villa of the Papyri belonged to Piso, whose family was prominent among the Roman aristocracy for several centuries. Though this is only a theory, it is very probably true. Cicero has left a most unflattering portrait of Piso, who was one of his political enemies: *facie magis quam facetis ridiculus* ("his face was funnier than his jokes"), he wrote in one of his letters. In fact, Piso was a learned and artistic nobleman and undoubtedly had greater political insight than Cicero himself: here is an example of the way in which archaeology can help to correct a biased judgement handed down in the written sources.

The Villa of the Papyri is noteworthy for yet another reason. As we have said, the methods of excavation used in the 18th century were deplorable. At Herculaneum tunnels were dug through the mass of petrified volcanic mud covering the ancient town. "These tunnels," wrote A. Maiuri, "pierced at random and running in every direction, at every level, even cutting across the upper storeys of houses, had but one aim: to extract from the bowels of the earth anything of value that could be found, without the slightest interest in the buildings themselves, which seemed condemned to remain buried for ever." In the case of the Villa of the Papyri, however, Charles Weber took the trouble of making a detailed plan, which can still be used.

This was not an easy task since the building as a whole was never cleared. In this case the intelligence and care of a scholar were able to make up for the faulty excavation methods of the time.

Even more admirable was the work of Father Antonio Piaggio, who in 1753 invented an ingenious device whereby the scrolls of papyri could be suspended so as to unroll under their own weight and be read.

In 1765, however, the Villa of the Papyri had to be abandoned: carbon dioxide had invaded the galleries and threatened to asphyxiate the *cavamonti*, as the excavators were called. The excavations were interrupted and have only recently been resumed with modern techniques. As the villa was not completely explored in the earlier excavations, it probably still has much of interest to yield.

Excavations at Pompeii, on the other hand, continued without a break. A great impetus was given to the work in 1806 when the Bourbons were replaced on the throne of Naples by Joseph Bonaparte and then by Murat. Here the task was made easier by the fact that the ancient town was covered by a relatively light layer of ashes and pebbles which was fairly easy to remove. It was thus possible, during the first three decades of the century, to clear the whole of the forum and the principal public buildings surrounding it, as well as a number of private houses.

The first excavations in Rome

The success of the excavations at Pompeii encouraged archaeologists to tackle other sites, and a start was made with those parts of Rome that were not completely covered with modern buildings. Up to the beginning of the 19th century the great buildings of the former capital of the world were treated with little respect, even during the period when the influence of humanism was predominant. Apart from Pius II and Leo X (under the latter, Raphael was appointed Commissioner of Antiquities and worked out a systematic programme for recording and preserving ancient buildings), most of the Renaissance Popes unscrupulously sacrified them to their own building plans. No serious attempt was made to remove the rubble covering the ruins; any clearance work carried out aimed at destroying rather than restoring them. The Campo Vaccino, which covered the Roman Forum, was some 30 feet above the ancient level. From time to time a scholar would make suggestions for restoring the ruins, but along very academic lines that were quite out of touch with reality. The first proper excavations did not start until 1788; they were instigated by von Frendenheim, the Swedish Ambassador. The work was given official sanction for the first time by the Comte de Tournon, the Prefect representing the French Empire, who appointed Carlo Fea as Commissioner of Antiquities. Fea held this office for thirty years. Various parts of the Roman Forum and the Forum of Trajan were tackled, and it soom became evident that the hypotheses about their topography advanced by Ligorio and other Renaissance scholars had been quite mistaken.

Roman archaeology in 19th-century Italy

Excavations continued in Rome and Pompeii throughout the 19th century, unaffected by the political upheavals of the time. The Forum and the Palatine gradually became archaeological preserves protected from the destructive invasions of modern life. Pius VII arranged for the systematic clearing of the Forum, and its temples were restored one by one: first that of Castor, then those of Vesta and Saturn. Work on the Forum continued actively during the pontificate of Leo XII and up to 1835. It then began to slow down, finally coming to a halt in 1854. The Palatine became the next focus of archaeological research in Rome when Napoleon III, who had bought part of the hill where the Caesars once dwelt, entrusted its exploration to Pietro Rosa. To him we owe the discovery, in 1869, of a house that, though relatively small, was decorated with splendid frescoes; these have unfortunately deteriorated considerably over the years, despite efforts to preserve them. The leaden water pipes were inscribed with the name "Julia Augusta", which was that taken by Livia, the wife of Augustus, after her husband's death. Rosa therefore called it "The House of Livia" and identified it as the birthplace of Tiberius, which—according to Suetonius—was situated on the Palatine. More recently, G. Lugli brought forward evidence to show that it was in fact Augustus' own house which his successors had transformed into a museum. After the unification of Italy, Rosa was put in charge of the excavations at the Forum as well as those on the Palatine. By about 1880, the whole Forum had been cleared down to at least the level of the mediaeval paving. In the concluding years of the century, R. Lanciani became Commissioner of Roman Antiquities. While continuing the excavations, he assembled all the documents he could find on chance discoveries throughout the city in modern times. His extensive research made it possible to reconstruct the topography of ancient Rome in detail—the relief plan of the city made by P. Bigot on the basis of his findings is particularly noteworthy.

At Pompeii, the great impetus given to research by the Napoleonic regime was kept up by the Bourbons until about 1825. Subsequently there was a notable falling-off, though large sums were still being spent (7000 ducats a year between 1830 and 1840). Instead of following a methodical plan, excavations were carried out in a rather haphazard manner, usually for the entertainment of distinguished visitors. Interest centred on the private houses and especially on the paintings they contained; unfortunately nothing was done to preserve them and they soon faded once they had been brought to light. The most interesting fragments were removed to the Museum at Naples.

In 1861, following the union of the Two Sicilies with the Kingdom of Italy, Fiorelli was put in charge of the excavations. He was responsible for

2, 3, 4, 5 →

16

17

21

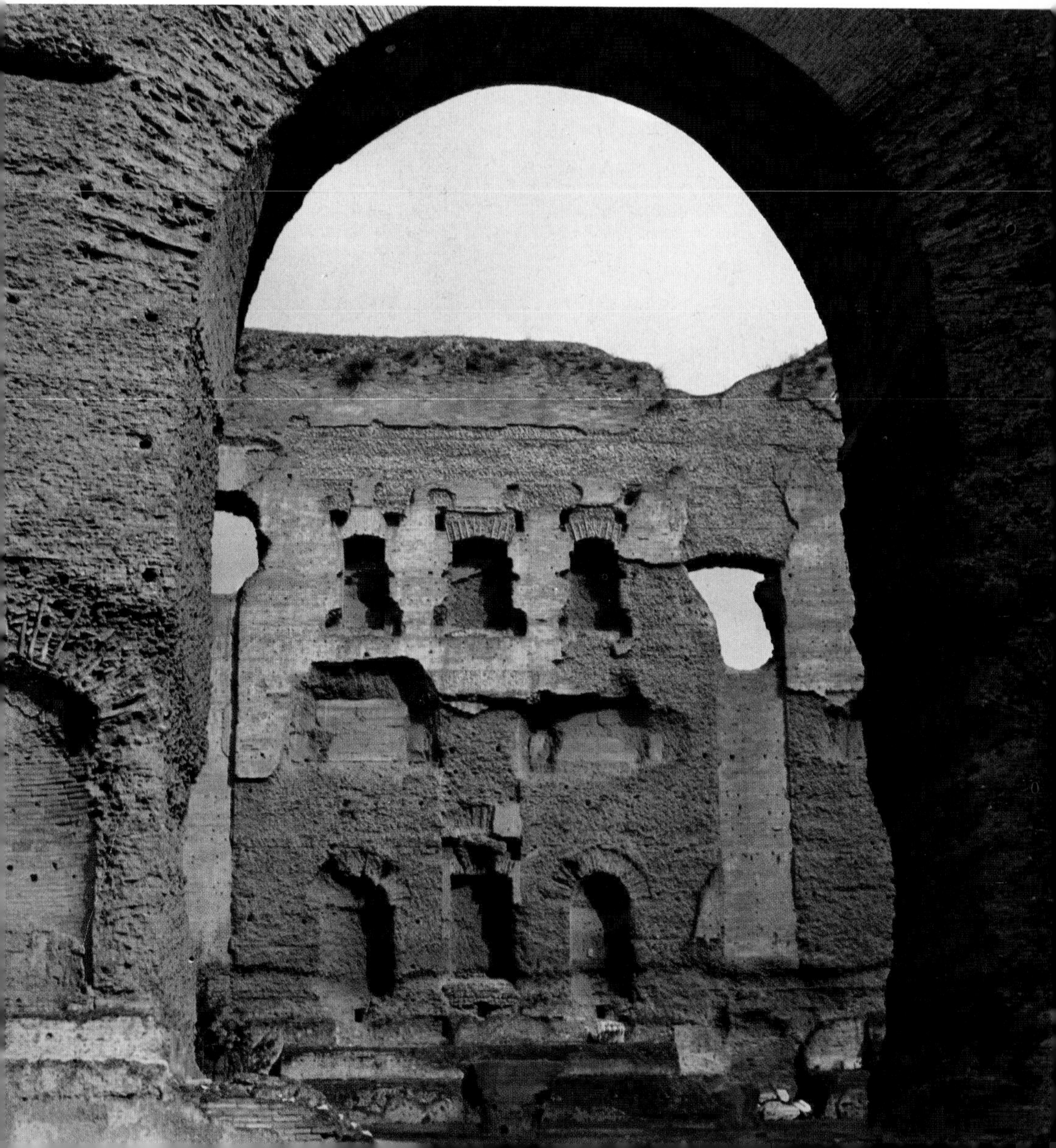

29

31

34

41

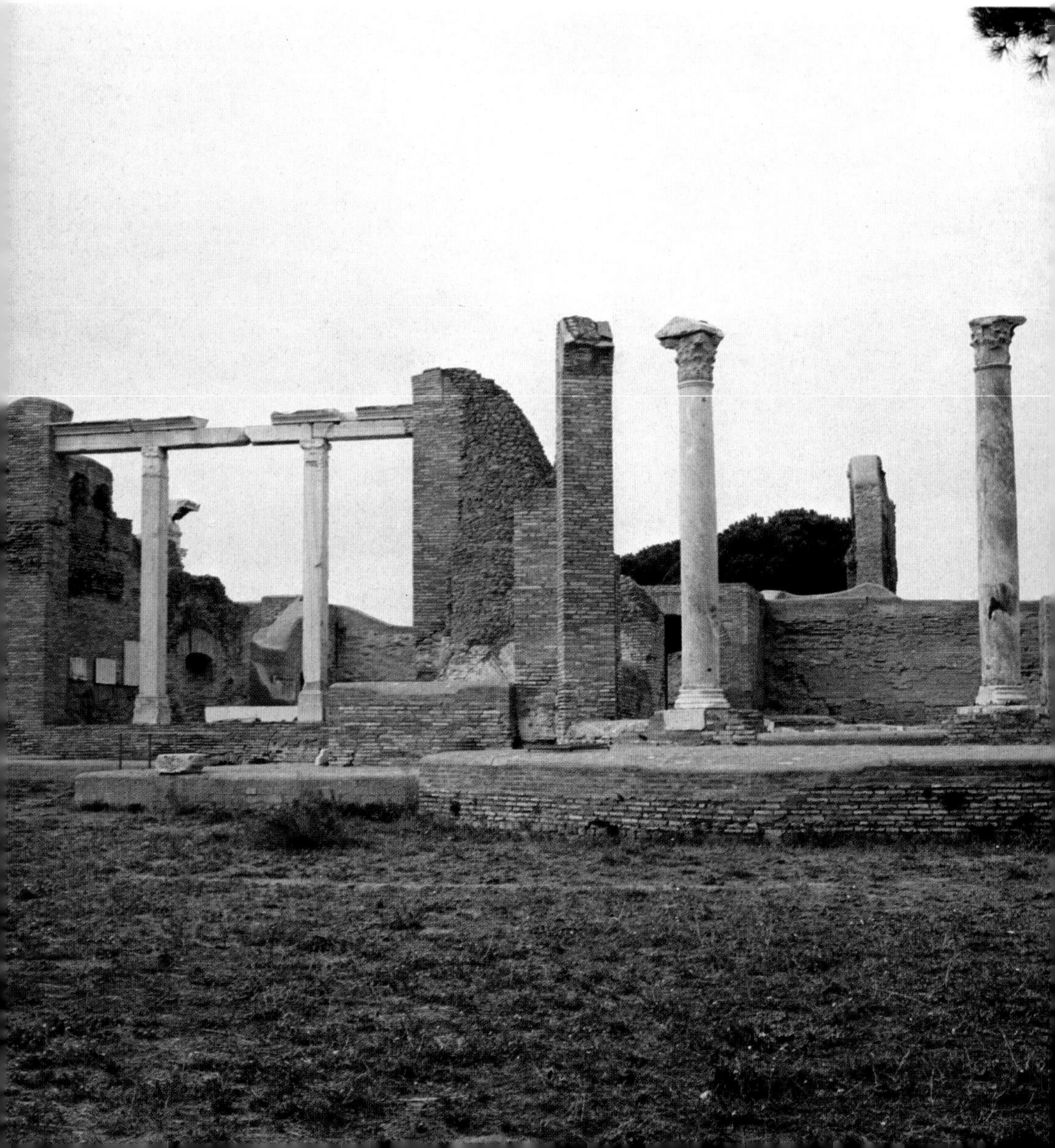

42

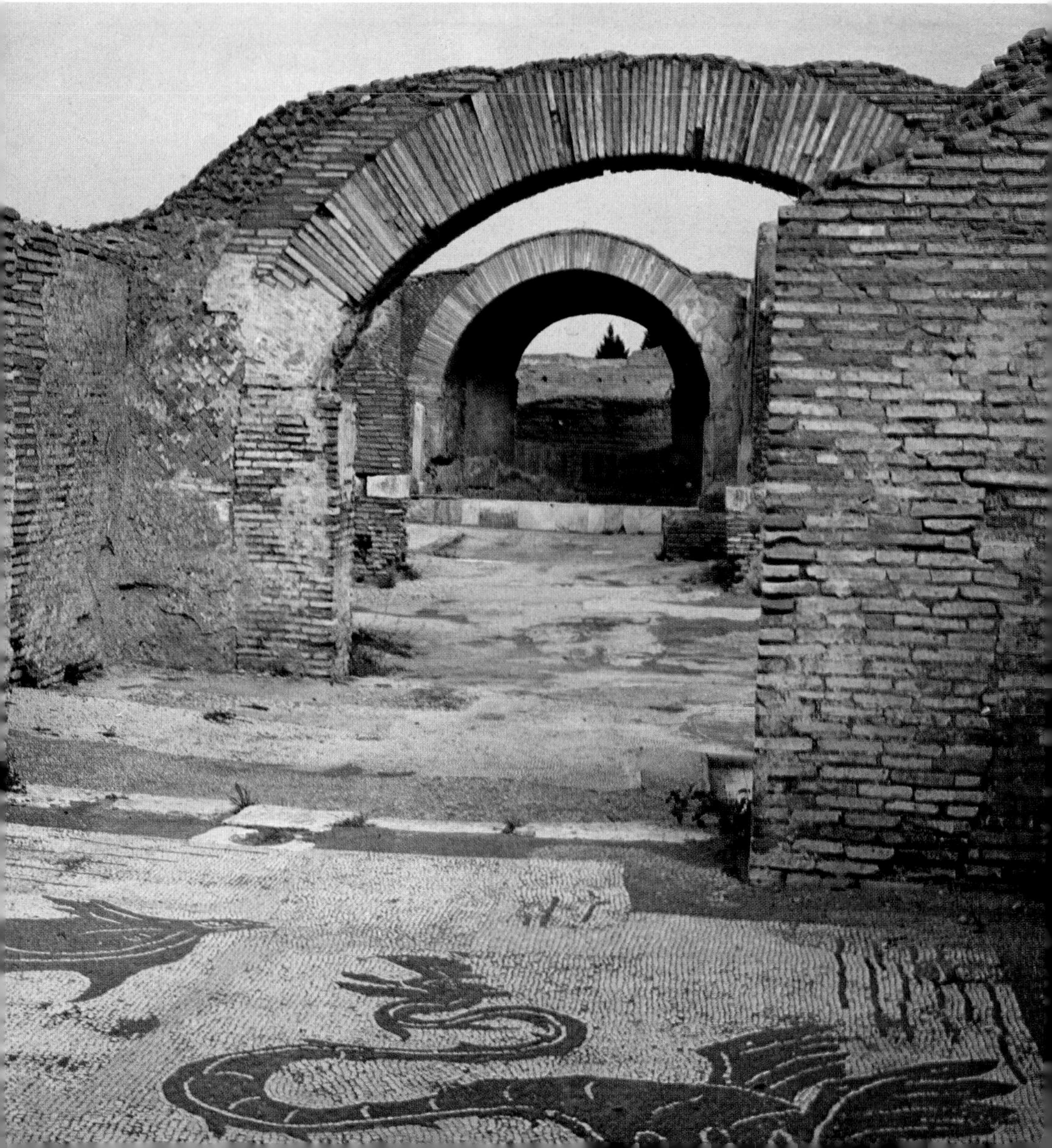

47

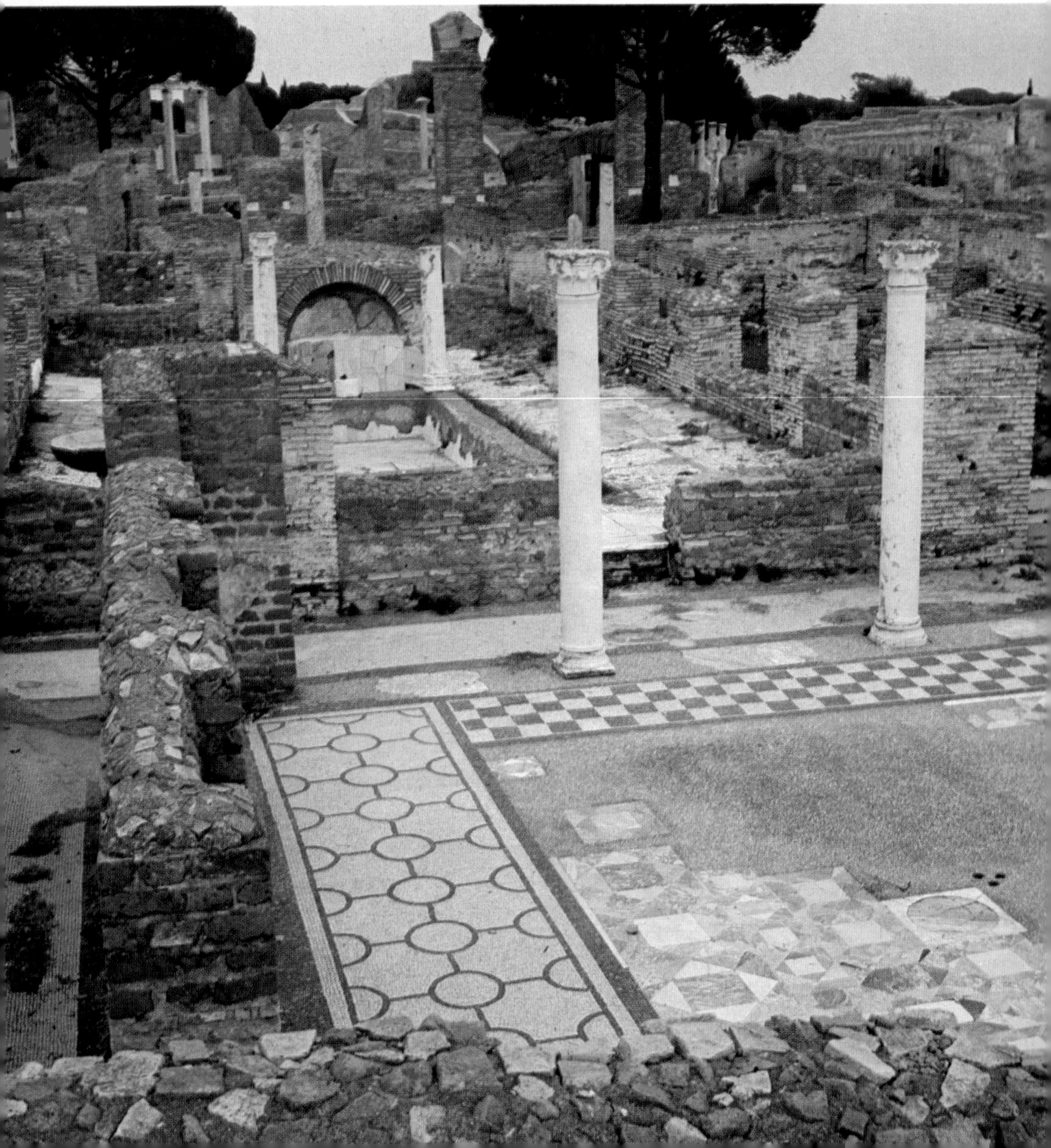

a vitally important technical innovation: until then, teams had moved the earth from the streets by cutting trenches, indiscriminately removing everything they encountered above the ancient ground-level, including collapsed parts of the façades and roofs of houses as well as the volcanic ash. Fiorelli was the first to order his team to dig the site horizontally, layer by layer, and to make a careful note of the items found at each level. He also took measures to prevent a "treasure hunt" for paintings, sculptures, and trinkets. Only in this way could the unity of the site as a whole be preserved, making it possible to gain a proper idea of the civilization of the period and its aesthetic tendencies.

Relative stagnation of Roman archaeology in the 19th century

Despite these achievements, the progress of Roman archaeology in the 19th century was not so rapid as that of many other sciences. In a number of countries, particularly France, it remained at the level of a "home industry" and was left in the hands of local scholars or architects. In spite of the example set in the last quarter of the century by Auguste Choisy, the translator and commentator of Vitruvius, these architects often used methods that showed a complete lack of any historical or critical sense. It is fortunate that their elegant but fanciful restorations remained on paper, for it would have been disastrous if they had been carried out.

This stagnation in the field of Roman archaeology in the 19th century is both puzzling and regrettable, since elsewhere archaeologists were resuscitating—first in Egypt and then in Mesopotamia—civilizations that had vanished completely. Even Greek studies were based at least as much on archaeology as on philology. Why did the Latinists hesitate to follow this example? Mainly, it seems, because of a misconception. In the 18th century, Winckelmann, "the father of classical archaeology", had set a low value on Roman art, and its originality only started to be appreciated round about

1890, when it was recognized by Wickhoff and the Viennese school. Thus, until quite recently, the inferiority of the Latin genius in art, as distinct from its creative ability in the realms of politics and law, was generally accepted. Although the 19th-century archaeologist was no longer a mere searcher after beautiful objects, he was still barely distinguishable from the art historian. As a result, Latinists found themselves more attracted to epigraphy, a discipline allied to history. In the second half of the 19th century, thousands of Latin inscriptions were dicovered and classified systematically in the Corpus published from 1863 onwards under the auspices of the Berlin Academy. Under the aegis of Mommsen—the great figure who dominated Latin studies in the last three decades of the century—scholars from every civilized nation reconstructed the administrative system of the early Empire with the aid of this new material. Literary texts had thrown practically no light on this system, whose perfect organization—which a modern state well might envy—was justly admired.

The achievements of 19th-century epigraphy would have been even more laudable if they had not resulted in the relegation of archaeology to a comparatively minor place. Mommsen and—in France—Cagnat encouraged their students to study inscriptions. In this field, which at first sight may appear rather a dull one, the student can sometimes receive that revelation of absolute truth—albeit in a limited sphere—that is so rarely granted to the historian. The discovery of a fine *cursus* may enable the career of a statesman or high official to be reconstructed down to its smallest details; on the other hand, it is much rarer to know something about his actual appearance, or that of his house or tomb. Unfortunately, when there was an opportunity to learn anything of this sort, it was invariably neglected. We have already spoken of Comparetti's theory that the Villa of the Papyri at Herculaneum was one of the summer residences of the Calpurnii Pisones. Unlike most of the other noble houses of Rome, this famous senatorial family survived until the 2nd and 3rd centuries A.D. In 1885 a funerary hypogeum, in which several of its members had been buried, was discovered near the Porta Pia in Rome. It contained altars inscribed with the names of the dead and ten magnificent carved sarcophagi. This discovery was as important to the student of Rome as the discovery of a Pharaoh's tomb would be to an Egyptologist. The sarcophagi were dispersed: two of them are in the Museo dei Termi in Rome, while seven others came—by way of a private collection—to the Walters Art Gallery at Baltimore in the United States. Admittedly they were discussed in a paper by K. Lehmann-Hartleben and E.C. Olsen, but not until 1942. Yet they constitute not only highly valuable works of art but also sources of the highest importance for the history of religion in the Roman Empire. As for the general history of the Calpurnii Pisones, who played such a prominent part in the affairs of the Empire for several centuries, no-one has yet attempted to write it.

Roman archaeology outside Europe

Roman archaeology would have been in an even poorer state had it not been for the expansion of the Empire along the African and Asiatic coasts of the Mediterranean. Some explanation is needed of the vestiges of Latin civilization—as well-preserved as those on the slopes of Vesuvius—that have been found in areas now dominated and transformed by Islam. Under the Flavian, Antonine, and Severan emperors (A.D. 79–235), North Africa, Syria, and Asia Minor reached a far higher level of prosperity than the European provinces. Methodical exploitation of the soil enabled a very dense population to live in regions that have now mostly reverted to steppe country inhabited only by nomad shepherds. While being dependent on agriculture for their basic livelihood, the peoples of Proconsular Africa and Numidia were not dispersed in villages but grouped in small towns— each with a few thousand inhabitants—standing some three to six miles apart. Conditions were similar in Asia Minor. In Tripolitania and the Syrian desert, on the other hand, the wealth of the inhabitants was derived chiefly from trade and the population was concentrated in large desert-surrounded towns with sumptuous public buildings.

The farmers and merchants were able to live and work only under military protection. The frontier lands were defended either by ramparts and continuous moats or by rings of camps and forts. In the course of the 3rd century, these defences began to give way under the assault of barbarian hordes who were sometimes driven on by others even more savage than themselves. The settled populations were gradually submerged, but this phenomenon did not occur everywhere in the same way. In eastern North Africa, the Ifrikia of the Arabs, for instance, the old conditions of life continued more or less unchanged under the first Moslem dynasties; it was the Hillanian invasion in the 11th century A.D. that finally destroyed the irrigation systems, thus putting an end to agriculture and depopulating towns whose inhabitants had, in any case, for the most part been massacred or driven to flight. In Syria, most of the "caravan cities" were wiped out—directly or indirectly—by the struggle between the Roman Empire and the various Iranian kingdoms. Dura Europos, for instance, was sacked by the Persians in 256, while Palmyra, the most important of these merchant towns, was attacked by the Romans themselves in 273 for having sought its independence. From our point of view, all these events had the same effect as the eruption of Vesuvius: the cities were suddenly abandoned at the height of their prosperity and never reoccupied. Others died a slow death, but their last inhabitants—with larger premises than they needed and very limited technical resources—left the buildings in which they camped practically untouched. In these arid regions great masses of sand, carried by wind or water, quickly settle round anything that breaks the general flatness of the landscape. Thus most of the ruins were soon wrapped in a thick protective mantle.

Africa: Timgad (Plates 50-55)

From the 18th century on, most of the dead cities of Africa and the East were visited and described by European travellers. But the first scientific exploration had to await the French conquest of Algeria. Although Bruce, a Scottish traveller, had drawn attention to Timgad—also known as the

"African Pompeii"—in 1765, it was not until 1851 that it was first visited by the epigraphist L. Renier. Another thirty years passed before any systematic excavation was undertaken. Even then, the work was left too much in the hands of the architects whose restorations admittedly saved the ruins from complete destruction but were not preceded by a sufficiently careful study of the buildings. The centre of the city, built on the orders of Trajan in 100 A.D., chiefly impresses us with the regularity of its ground plan. It is subdivided into regular blocks by straight streets cutting one another at right angles. The site—a bare and monotonous high plain lying north of the Aures—favoured this lay-out, which recalls the designs of the military engineers for the famous camps of the legionaries. This was, in fact, a frontier zone, and the settlers—established by Minucius Natalis, the Imperial Legate—were the veterans of Augustus' Third Legion, the elite of the African army. The permanent barracks of this unit were at Lambese, 16 miles farther west; they too have been partly cleared, though one section is unfortunately covered by a modern prison. From the 2nd century on, the pacification of the region stretching to the south of the Aures finally permitted the citizens of Timgad to lead the quiet, easy life enjoyed by other citizens of the Empire. The population grew, and suburbs developed along the approach roads. These contained luxurious community buildings, such as the baths and the magnificently equipped "spa" discovered only twenty years ago inside the ramparts of a Byzantine fortress. To the benefits of agriculture were added those of trade, to which the presence of several market-places bears witness. The elegant library shows that there was a thriving intellectual life. But the inhabitants of Timgad—like all Africans— were mainly preoccupied by religious questions. After following the cults of the Punic tradition—in particular that of Saturn—until the end of the 2nd century, they underwent a mass conversion to Christianity. The presence of several churches—all of them in the suburbs—recalls the bitter divisions among the faithful, the majority of whom probably went over to the typically African Donatist sect, led by the dynamic Bishop Optat, in the 4th century.

Despite its present fame, it should be remembered that Timgad occupied a relatively minor place among the Roman towns of Africa, and that there are dozens of others still unexcavated. The excavation of Hippone, carried out over the last few years by E. Marec, shows how even well-known sites can conceal their treasures almost indefinitely. Twenty years ago the city forum with its intact paving—dating, according to an inscription, from the time of Vespasian—and St Augustine's Cathedral with all its ancillary buildings still lay buried under gardens, and there was nothing to suggest their presence there. Yet many attempts had been made to locate the basilica, and in the 19th century the clergy even took an action against the municipality to stop it putting water in the Roman cisterns which were erroneously believed to mark the site of the monastery founded by the saint. Even at Carthage, where excavations had been carried out by the White Fathers and the Tunisian Service of Antiquities since 1881, the best-preserved ancient building, the Baths of Antoninus *(Plates 56, 57)*, was not cleared until 1944.

As recently as 1960, road works brought to light the largest paving yet found in Carthage: measuring 40×26 feet, it has a pattern of 198 squares in which slabs of coloured marble alternate with mosaics depicting race-horses.

Tripolitania, as its name indicates, formerly contained only three cities, as compared with the hundreds in Tunisia and Algeria; but one of them—Leptis Magna *(Plate 68)*—had the distinction of being the birthplace of Septimius Severus (193–211 A.D.). This emperor endowed his native town with imposing buildings, including a forum and a basilica, which were rapidly engulfed by sand at the end of the classical era and were accordingly found in a good state of preservation. The Italian archaeologists who discovered them also restored the theatre at Sabratha *(Plate 65)*, the most westerly of the three towns of Tripolitania; this building, with its three storeys of superimposed colonnades, is undoubtedly one of the most magnificent examples of ancient baroque architecture.

Syria

The archaeological riches of North Africa are so great that it would take centuries of work, backed by vast financial resources, to bring them all to light. But Syria has quite as many sites, and its monuments are even more impressive. For example, there is the well-known group of three temples at Baalbek *(Plates 60, 61);* built over a period of two and a half centuries (1st–3rd centuries A.D.), they achieve a remarkable synthesis of Roman architectural and aesthetic principles and ancient Semitic traditions. Since the beginning of this century, the work at Baalbek has been carried on mainly by German archaeologists. Taking advantages of the good political relations between the German and Ottoman Empires, the Germans also started systematic excavations at Palmyra, under the direction of T. Wiegand, before the First World War; this work was continued in the inter-war period by French scholars attached to the Syrian-Lebanese Department of Antiquities, and today it is being carried on by a Polish team. Farther south, in Jordan, the splendid sites of Gerasa and Petra are now the preserve of American archaeologists.

Dura Europos

In the inter-war period, it fell to the Americans, in collaboration with the French, to carry out the most spectacular excavations in the Near East. Dura Europos occupied a strategic and commercially favourable position on the Euphrates, at the boundaries of Syria and northern Mesopotamia. At the end of the 4th century B.C. it was colonized by a group of Macedonian veterans who were settled there by King Seleucus I, formerly one of Alexander's generals. A halt for caravans carrying Chinese silk to the West, the town subsequently fell under the domination of the Kingdom of Parthia, while in economic and cultural matters it was greatly influenced by Palmyra. Finally, at the beginning of the 2nd century A.D., Dura was occupied by the Romans and became a frontier post defending the Empire against the Parthians. It was destroyed in 256 by the army of the new Sassanid dynasty, under which Persian nationalism had been revived. For several centuries, therefore, Dura was a crossroads of the Greek, Latin, Semitic, and Iranian cultures. The suddenness with which it was abandoned and the dryness of the climate ensured its preservation in conditions equalled only in Herculaneum and Pompeii.

In 1920, a French frontier officer accidentally discovered a half-ruined wall decorated with splendidly preserved paintings of a religious ceremony. The newly formed Syrian-Lebanese Department of Antiquities was alerted. The discovery was also reported to two world-renowned scholars with a special interest in Syria: F. Cumont, a Belgian, whose main field of study was the spread of mystic religions from the East throughout the Roman Empire, and Rostovtzeff, a Russian émigré, who had carried out research on the caravan cities. On the advice of these scholars, the Franco-American missions were organized. The results were spectacular: the town walls were found just as they had been at the moment of the attack of 256; the corpses of the combatants were still lying in their trenches, with their weapons, clothes, and personal belongings. Persian and Greek temples dedicated to the Palmyrian gods, a synagogue, and even a Christian church—the oldest known—were unearthed. They were decorated with frescoes testifying to the strange religious ferment that stirred the outposts of the Asiatic and Mediterranean world in the first centuries of the Christian era. Dura Europos may be termed a Pompeii of the desert, but a later Pompeii with an entirely different culture.

Antioch

Round about the same time, other Franco-American missions were looking for the remains of Antioch, which was the capital of one of the Macedonian kingdoms that came into being following the dismemberment of Alexander's empire, and the chief town of Syria until the Middle Ages. They hoped to

56

57

58 —

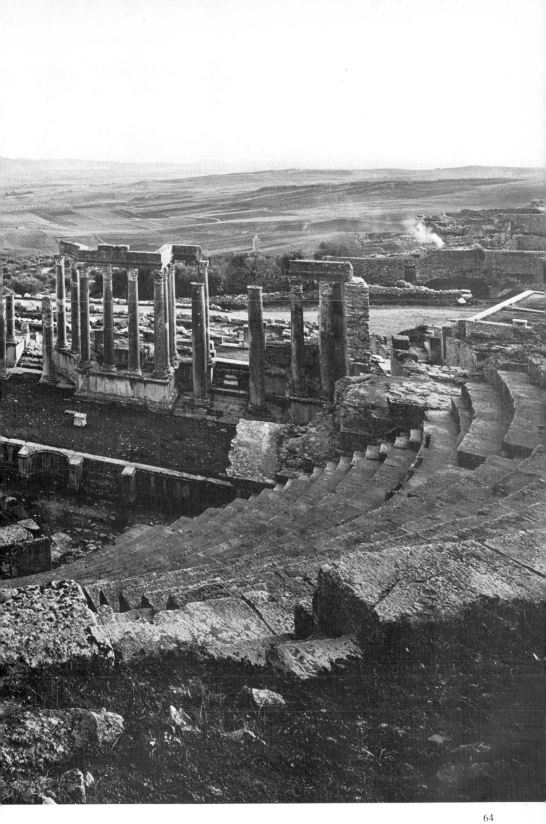

65,66

discover the remains of the Hellenistic metropolis, but, as it turned out, nearly all the finds were connected with Roman Antioch. There, as so often elsewhere, the great prosperity of the Imperial era had, quite naturally and without any violence, led to the obliteration of remains from earlier periods. The houses of the Roman period were themselves almost entirely razed to the ground, but their mosaic floors constitute a body of evidence whose equivalent can be found only in Italy and North Africa.

Asia Minor

At the beginning of the 20th century, German and Austrian missions—again, thanks to the alliance between the Central Powers and Turkey—undertook the systematic exploration of the ancient cities of Asia Minor. This work has since been continued by other foreign teams and by the Turkish Government, but it is still far from being finished. In this region the vestiges of earlier periods are undoubtely of much more interest than those of the Empire; nevertheless, the baths and the library at Ephesus (the latter has a monumental façade with sculptures glorifying the Antonine dynasty), the theatre at Ephesus, the theatre at Aspendus (whose stage has been preserved intact), and the baths at Miletus are among the most imposing examples of Roman architecture. These Anatolian towns, like those of Syria, are especially noteworthy for the breadth and magnificence of their town-planning. The streets lined with porticos are on a particularly impressive scale; one of them, discovered at Apamea by Belgian archaeologists, has been taken to Brussels and reconstructed at the Musée du Cinquantenaire.

The progress of archaeology in Italy: the beginnings of Rome

European nations have, paradoxically, generally attached more importance to their overseas archaeological expeditions than to excavations on their own territories. In Italy, however, great progress has been made since the beginning of the 20th century. According to the Roman historians—Livy, in particular—the future capital of Rome was founded on the Palatine by Romulus in 753 B.C. and ruled over for two and a half centuries by seven kings, the last three being of Etruscan origin. Nineteenth-century historians tended to regard such accounts as legendary asserting that nothing definite was known of the history of Rome before the capture of the city by the Gauls at the beginning of the 4th century B.C. However, when Boni was examining the basement of the Palace of the Flavians on the Palatine, he found traces of stakes and fragments of clay coating from huts. In 1907, farther to the west on the same hill, near a temple of Cybele, Vagliesi discovered drainage canals that had belonged to a protohistoric village. In 1948, the foundations of huts were found carved in the tufa on the same site. In the meantime, Boni had made a further discovery, in the Forum near the Temple of Antoninus, of some forty tombs where the ashes of the dead were contained in urns that were tiny replicas of the huts in which they had lived. It was thus possible to reconstruct these dwellings exactly: they were made of clay-covered thatch and supported by a wooden framework. The material contained in these tombs and in the huts can be dated in relation to that found on other sites: it seems most probable that it goes back to the middle of the 8th century B.C., i.e., the very period when, according to tradition, Romulus and Remus settled on the Palatine. This work was taken up again in recent years and has enabled the Danish scholar, E. Gjerstadt, to propose a precise chronology for the first few centuries of Rome; this has not, however, been universally accepted. Nevertheless, we now have indisputable evidence supporting, in its broad outlines, the traditional account of the birth of Rome.

According to the Romans, Romulus' own tomb was situated on the Forum, not far from the Curia. It was Boni again who, in 1899, excavated beneath the "black stone" covering the hallowed spot: he found traces of a tomb, but they were of a period about four centuries later than that of Romulus. Lower down, he found a *cippus* bearing the oldest Latin inscription known to us; part of it has remained a mystery to this day despite every effort of the philologists to elucidate it.

The resurrection of Pompeii

At Pompeii, too, noteworthy progress was made in the early 20th century. While the hot ashes of the eruption destroyed all organic matter, the forms they covered survived. Fiorelli was the first to think of pouring plaster into the hollows left by the victims' bodies; he thus obtained a touching, though macabre, series of casts which greatly impress the tourists *(Plates 9, 10)*. Subsequently the same technique was used for wooden objects, doors, furniture, staircases, and the balustrades of balconies; it even made it possible to determine the species of the trees in the gardens. In the closing years of the 19th century it began to be realized that it might be desirable to preserve the decorations and contents of houses where they were, instead of moving the "fine pieces" to the Museum at Naples and leaving the remainder to inevitable destruction. One of the first houses to benefit from this new policy was the House of the Vettii—rich merchants who had had the frescoes on their walls entirely redone after the earthquake of 63 A.D., the first warning of the catastrophe that was to annihilate the town. This was during the reign of Nero, an emperor who—though later much discredited— was undoubtedly a connoisseur and launched fashions that his subjects were quick to follow, whether or not they approved of his policies. The frescoes in the House of the Vettii were thus influenced by those commissioned by Nero for his own palace, the legendary House of Gold (Domus Aurea). Most of them are still in place; admittedly they have had to be restored and this is sometimes all too evident, but techniques are constantly improving in this field and even the most exacting art-lover will find no fault with the more recently discovered frescoes. In 1912 V. Spinazzola was appointed Superintendent of Antiquities in Campania. He decided to concentrate on one of the main streets of Pompei, the Via dell' Abbondanza *(Plate 7)*. This is a wide, straight thoroughfare that starts at the forum and runs north-east to the Sarno Gate. Perfecting Fiorelli's technique, Spinazzola not only had the earth cleared in layers, but also forbade the removal of any object or fragment encountered, taking steps to strengthen them before the digging was resumed. By this painstaking method the upper parts of the houses were restored as the excavation proceeded, whereas previously they had, at best, been reconstructed only after first being demolished. Bit by bit the ancient street took on its true aspect; thus it was learnt that Roman houses were not—as had previously been supposed— completely isolated from the outside, with inner courtyards as the sole source of light and air. On the contrary, at least the upper storeys had wide bay-windows, balconies, and loggias. The ground-floor façades were decorated with paintings in warm colours—geometrical designs or, more usually, representations of family gods or the scenes from everyday life that frequently served as signs for merchants or craftsmen. Spinazzola also took great care to restore the interior decoration and the gardens. It was he who saved the charming House of Octavius Quartio with its wide loggia opening on a fine garden where water from a richly ornate fountain once splashed down to a marble-lined canal. This garden, like several others, has even been replanted. A number of attempts were made in the 19th century to reopen the excavations at Herculaneum which, as we have seen, had been abandoned in 1765. But each time the archaeologists were discouraged by the difficulties involved. It was not until Mussolini intervened in 1927 that the necessary funds for a systematic exploration were forthcoming. Several districts have now been cleared completely, and are being treated with the same care as the remains at Pompeii: paintings are preserved on the spot, works of art are replaced by exact replicas, furnishings, roofs, balconies, even ropes and baskets, are being reconstituted exactly as they were on the day of the eruption.

Ostia (Plates 32-49)

Herculaneum and Pompeii were mainly pleasure centres, corresponding to our own holiday resorts. Ostia, the port of Rome, was more the equivalent of one of our industrial and commercial cities. Ruined at the beginning of the

Middle Ages, it owes its preservation to the fact that malaria kept it deserted until 1909. Systematic clearing operations were then started and they have continued uninterruptedly ever since; the main guiding spirit of the work was G. Calza, who died a few years ago. Ostia enables us to visualize Imperial Rome at the height of its power, with its many-storeyed apartment buildings, its huge warehouses, its temples open to worshippers from all over the world. The frescoes (generally later than those at Pompeii) and the splendid black-and-white mosaics (a speciality of the Italian school) are particularly noteworthy. However, from the end of the 3rd century on, the city's economic activity declined and its warehouses were replaced by the seaside villas of noble Roman families.

The Imperial Fora (Plates 11-18)

In Rome itself, the Fascist government promoted archaeological research on a large scale. We do not need to go into its motives for doing so. Professional archaeologists generally did not share them and did not relish using methods more concerned with producing an effect than with scientific objectivity and integrity. We are right to deplore the demolition of many Renaissance and 17th-century buildings and to feel sorry that delightful old districts were sacrificed to make way for the vast, lifeless Via del Impero. Nevertheless, we must admit that the clearing of the Imperial Fora—the Forum of Julius Caesar, the Forum of Augustus, and especially the Forum of Trajan—has made a great contribution to our knowledge of the past, as well as providing an impressive group of monuments at the foot of the Capitoline. On the other side of the sacred hill, at the Campus Martius, a whole section of Republican Rome was revealed at the same time as the four temples of the Largo Argentina. Beside the Tiber, the old pillared Shrine of Apollo is now revealed in front of the Theatre of Marcellus which has been partly cleared of the surrounding hovels. In the same area, clearance work for new streets brought to light temples that in some cases go back to the time of the Etruscan kings. The archaeological work of the Fascist period, at its best and worst, reached its peak in 1937 with the "Mostra Augustea della Romanità" organized on the occasion of the bimillenary of the birth of Augustus in 63 B.C.—an ironical tribute in a way, when we think of the gulf separating the prudence and cunning of the first Emperor from the bombast of the Duce. But at least it offered a valuable opportunity for assembling casts from all parts of the Empire. This unique collection has not been dispersed, and it now forms the Museum of Roman Civilization.

Excavations of frontier areas. Aerial photography

Germany was the first European nation to organize a methodical search for the Roman remains in its territory. In 1892, an international congress decided to undertake a systematic study of the frontier areas of the Roman Empire.

At the end of the 1st century B.C., the Emperor Augustus had devised a plan for protecting the whole Mediterranean world by means of a vast line of fortifications manned by all the forces of the imperial army. This system made it possible for a comparatively small number of professional soldiers (a little over 300,000 men) to safeguard the peace of several million individuals. For two hundred years, it was the principal means of securing the prosperity and well-being of the Empire and, though shaken by the invasions at the end of the 2nd century, it continued to be relatively effective for almost as long again, for after each rupture the breaches were filled in and new posts were set up.

The archaeological study of the frontier areas was first undertaken in Germany. In the 2nd century, the defence line in that part of Europe followed the lower Rhine, from its mouth to Coblenz; it then crossed to the right bank of the river, continuing to the upper Danube on the Regensburg side,

Baden, Württemberg, and southern Bavaria being thus enclosed within the Empire. The various traces of ramparts—for several lines were constructed at intervals between the reign of Vespasian (69–79) and the end of the 2nd century, taking in a larger part of the Germanic countries each time—were examined in the greatest detail. The army posts forming the skeleton of the frontier system were excavated, and some—like the Saalburg in the Taunus range—were reconstructed in impressive fashion.

Similar work has been carried out in England and Scotland, along the two walls by which Hadrian and Antoninus isolated the wild north of the island. It was also in Great Britain that the first collection of archaeological photographs taken from the air was published by O.G.S. Crawford in 1939. Shortly afterwards R.P. Poidebard used the same technique when searching for Roman remains in the Syrian desert. Aerial photography was also used by Colonel Baradez, from 1940 on, to trace the Roman fortifications on the fringe of the Sahara, where he discovered not only military remains but also fossilized traces of agriculture whose presence in this desert area seems strange to us today.

Great contemporary excavations: the Crypt of St Peter's

Since the nineteen-thirties, Roman archaeology has made spectacular progress everywhere, and has aroused great public interest. In Italy, not only is work proceeding on the great traditional sites, but new sites are being opened up. Some have been entrusted to foreign expeditions, such as the Institut Belge de Rome, which is excavating the ruins of a 3rd-century B.C. Roman colony at Alba Fucens in the heart of the Apennines. In Rome itself, on 28 June 1938, Pope Pius XII ordered an examination of the foundations of St Peter's in order to verify the authenticity of the tradition that the tomb of the Apostle was situated under the high altar of the basilica. These excavations continued for ten years, all through the political cataclysm that shook the world and threatened to destroy Rome itself. They certainly surpass all others in the importance of their aim, the grandeur of their setting, and the interest of their results. First of all, they revealed the best-preserved Roman necropolis known to us. Constantine's basilica, which preceded the building designed by Michelangelo, was erected on the site of a cemetery where Roman families had buried their dead for several centuries. Starting in a small way in the second half of the 1st century, this cemetery later developed into what might be termed "a city of the dead", with row upon row of monumental mausoleums decorated with marble and mosaics. One section, at a somewhat higher level than the rest of the cemetery, was approached by a ramp supported by walls; the stamp on the tiles covering one of the conduits showed that it dated back to the time of Marcus Aurelius (160–180 A.D.). In one of the supporting walls—the "red wall"—was built the small memorial that, in the reign of Constantine, would determine the site for the most famous of Western churches. This was a simple niche hollowed out of the wall and decorated with a plain stone altar supported by two marble columns. It obviously dates from the last thirty years of the second century, i.e., from between the building of the "red wall" and the year 200 when the "trophy" of St Peter was first mentioned by Gaius the priest. When the Christians of the period erected this monument—the best their humble means permitted—did they know for certain that it marked the spot where the tortured remains of the founder of their Church had been laid to rest a hundred years earlier? The excavations have unfortunately furnished no definite answer to this question, although 1st-century tombs were found in the proximity of the niche. At all events, it is probable that the relics of St Peter were taken to the catacombs in the 3rd century, to be protected from the enemies of the Church, and brought back to the Vatican only a short time before the building of the Basilica.

The villa in Piazza Armerina (Plates 120-125)

From the founder of the Catholic Church, we must now turn to one of his most formidable enemies. During the nineteen-thirties excavations were re-opened on a site in the centre of Sicily, near Piazza Armerina, in the hope that it would yield material for the Mostra Augustea. This site had long been known, but it had not yet been systematically explored. The delay was fortunate, for it would have been impossible in the 19th century—and even at the beginning of the 20th—to preserve the outstanding group of mosaics discovered there in the ruins of a magnificent villa dating from the end of the Empire. One of these—showing young girls in "bikinis"—is widely known for its oddly modern air. But we should not, on that account, underestimate the mosaic showing the labours of Hercules, in which the monstrous bodies of giants with snake-shaped legs writhe in agony from the wounds inflicted by the hero's arrows—this work is comparable in its dramatic power to a fresco by Michelangelo. There is also a vast paving decorated with exotic hunting scenes featuring tigers, rhinoceroses, and hippopotami. Among the other noteworthy mosaics at the villa are some based on Greek myths, but most of them illustrate the luxurious, easy life of the great nobles who, in this period of transition, enjoyed not only the comforts and culture of the ancients but also a power anticipating that of the medieval barons. Who was the fortunate owner of this princely estate? Shortly after its discovery, a Norwegian scholar H. L'Orange, suggested that it had belonged to the Emperor Maximianus Herculius. A former professional soldier, Maximianus owed his rank to his friendship with Diocletian, who, on becoming Emperor after a military *coup d'état*, chose him as associate (287 A.D.). This team—which later included two other colleagues of lower status and was accordingly known as the Tetrarchy—reigned until 305, when Diocletian abdicated and Maximianus had to follow suit, rather against his will. An attempt to seize power again some time later led to his violent and mysterious death at the court of his son-in-law, Constantine. L'Orange believed that he used the palace at Piazza Armerina during his few years of retirement.

Unfortunately, L'Orange's brilliant theory has recently been discredited since the style of the mosaics indicate that the palace cannot have been built earlier than the middle of the fourth century; it most probably belonged to one of those rich senators who for a long time continued to defend the cause of dying paganism.

Roman archaeology in present-day France

The fall of Napoleon III meant the end of the work—remarkable for its time—that had been undertaken under his direction at Alesia, Saint-Germain, and elsewhere. The special place of the "Gallic myth" in the ideology of the Third Republic subsequently delayed research into the Imperial period. It was not until 1942, at the instigation of the Latinist J. Carcopino, that an embryonic archaeological service was created in France, although it was less well-equipped than the corresponding service in Italy and even than those in the French overseas territories, colonies, and protectorates. A new archaeological administration is now being organized by André Malraux. In 1941, the first Gallo-Roman excavations to employ truly scientific methods were started at Saint-Rémy-de-Provence, under the direction of H. Rolland. There, over the next twenty years or so, the ruins of Glanum *(Plate 69)*—a small town situated at the exit of a pass in the Alpilles, beside a mineral spring deified by the Celt-Ligurians—were brought to light. Hellenized under the influence of Marseilles, conquered and rebuilt by the Romans, Glanum was already noted for two magnificent ancient buildings: a triumphal arch and a mausoleum. It was a complete surprise, however, when a forum surrounded by houses and temples—the best-preserved dating from the end of the 1st century B.C.—was unearthed to the south of these monuments. This is the only place in France where you can walk through the centre of an ancient town that is almost as well preserved as those discovered in Italy, Africa, or the East; its splendid setting is an additional attraction. Before work started at Saint-Rémy, archaeologists had already been drawn to Vaison, which is situated below Mount Ventoux at the northern border of Provence; several districts of the ancient town have been cleared by Canon Sautel. While the civic centre has not been found, the luxury of the houses—which have unfortunately been over-zealously restored—testified to the wealth of the local aristocracy, to whom Burrhus, the prefect of Nero's praetorium, belonged. In addition to these exceptional sites, France contains a fair number of Roman buildings hemmed in by modern towns; efforts are now being made to restore them and clear away the surrounding houses. The most noteworthy work in this direction has been carried out in Paris (the Baths of Cluny), at Lyons (a theatre and Odeum), and especially at Arles where vast underground galleries dating from the Augustan period have regained their former splendour. North of the Loire, on the other hand, there are isolated rural sites, usually consisting of a richly decorated temple accompanied by a theatre. In classical times, there were centres for the rural inhabitants, who benefited more than one might think from the great prosperity of the Empire. At the moment, the archaelogical group of the French Touring Club is carrying out excavations on a remarkably well-preserved site of this kind at Génainville in the Vexin, some 25 miles from Paris, and several others are being carefully investigated.

Spanish sites: Ampurias (Plate 81) *and Italica* (Plates 78-80)

The archaeological wealth of Spain is equalled in Europe only by that of Italy. Of the sites of the Roman period, two in particular have been systematically explored. On the Catalan coast, the old Phocean colony of Ampurias was one of the most brilliant western centres of Hellenism in the six centuries preceding the Christian era, even though the Greek settlers lived in a closely confined aera surrounded by ramparts. It consisted of two districts (one on either side of the river) of which only the more recent has been cleared, the other remaining hidden under the old village of San Martín. In the older part of the town, the meanness of the houses—squeezed along the walls—and the dearth of public buildings are surprising. There was no real security for the inhabitants until Caesar's victory at Ilerda in 46 B.C., following which the town rapidly expanded. The palaces built after that date are as large and sumptuous as the finest senator's villas in Rome and testify to an extraordinarily rapid increase in the wealth of the local aristocracy. The site has been excavated methodically over the last quarter of a century under the direction of Professor M. Almagro.

In Andalusia, a few miles from what is now Seville, Scipio Africanus settled some of his veterans in a township which he called Italica. At the end of the 1st century one of the families settled there—the Ulpii—attained the highest rank when Trajan, whose father had been one of the foremost senators and generals of his time, ascended the throne of the Empire in 98 A.D. He was succeeded as emperor by his nephew Hadrian, an Aelius. Hadrian in particular took a great interest in his homeland: during his reign, the town was rebuilt in large rectangular blocks separated by straight streets and containing huge mansions whose conception and decoration were influenced by Roman tradition and Hellenistic fashion, as well as by local practices and the exigencies of the climate. Thus the entrance leads directly into the house, according to Roman custom (the Greeks preferred one that did not reveal the interior), with a kind of screen across the corridor to shield it from the eyes of the curious. These and many other points relating to Italica have been admirably dealt with by Professor A. García y Bellido, Director of the Spanish Institute of Archaeology, which has been specially concerned with this site.

Conimbriga

Lusitania, on the shores of the Atlantic, seemed to the Romans to lie at the edge of the universe. Civilization was first brought there during the Augustan period by the military settlers of Emerita—now Mérida—where a number of important Roman monuments survive, although most of the original town has been covered by modern buildings. In due course, the local inhabitants discovered the pleasures of *urbanitas* for themselves. This is particularly evident at Conimbriga, whose closeness to the famous University of Coimbra has helped to make it a favourite site for Portuguese archaeologists. Increasingly intensive excavations since 1930 have brought to light there—as elsewhere—houses and public buildings, such as baths, that testify to the comfort enjoyed by rich and poor alike under Roman rule. The interior decoration is noteworthy, the floors being of particular interest, with their mosaics based on models current throughout the Empire, yet treated with a naïvety that shows how local craftsmen failed to understand classical aesthetics, though at the same time it demonstrates their strong individuality.

Central Europe

The reign of Trajan (98–117) marks a turning point in Roman policy in Europe: in the military field, attention was focused on the Rhine and the Danube, where forces were considerably strengthened. As the army was not only a means of defence but also one of the most active agents of the Empire in the economic and even the cultural field, this led to a great development of the frontier provinces. These coincided more or less with the present territories of Switzerland, Austria, Hungary, Yugoslavia, and Rumania, in all of which important excavations are now in progress. In Switzerland, the best explored site is that of the former Augusta Raurica on the outskirts of Basel; since the end of the 19th century, the central district of this settlement—founded by Munatius Plancus at the same time as Lyons in 44 B.C.—has been systematically excavated. The work has revealed a town with a plan as symmetrical as that of Timgad. The *forum*—now completely cleared—is similar in lay-out to the Forum of Trajan in Rome: a basilica with two apses stands on one of the shorter sides, while the other is occupied by a secular temple. This lay-out, found in many of the towns of Gaul and Britain—for instance, at Silchester—must have been employed systematically throughout the western provinces at the beginning of the 2nd century. Ruined by the Alamanni in the 3rd century, Augusta Raurica was replaced by a *castrum*, or fortified village, which has survived to this day under the name of Kaiseraugst . It was there that Professor Laur Belart discovered one of the richest hoards of 4th-century silver that has yet come to light *(Plates 132, 134)*; the largest item is a dish engraved with the legend of Achilles.

The Austrian Archaeological Institute, which has done much important work in the Balkans and the Near East, is also in charge of excavations in its own country. The most important sites, those of Virunum and Teurnia, lie in the territory of the former Celtic kingdom of Noricum, which was attached to the Empire by Augustus and corresponds to present-day Carinthia.

The Hungarian and Croatian plains south of the Danube formed the region known as Pannonia. There are three reasons why the civilization of the Empire took such firm root there: the agricultural wealth of the region: the size of the military occupation force (five legions distributed over two provinces from the time of Trajan onwards), which was, as elsewhere, an agent of progress favouring the social and political advancement of the local inhabitants (the Hungarian scholar A. Alföldi mentions a *Pannonier-herrschaft*, i.e., a predominance of Pannonians in the government of the Empire, towards the middle of the 3rd century A.D.); and, finally, the intersection of two great trading routes, one skirting the Danube and bringing men and ideas from the East, the other running to North Italy, where Aquileia already played a part similar to that of Venice at a later date. The region was also densely populated, especially in the vicinity of Lake Neusiedl, south of Carnuntum, in the bend of the Danube round Aquincum, on the northern shore of Lake Balaton, and at the point where the Drava and the

Sava flow into the plain. Outside the towns, which developed near the frontier posts (Aquincum and Carnuntum) or crossroads (Gorsium), the peasantry—many of whom were of Celtic origin—formed communities round the sumptuous country villas, as in Gaul. The Budapest Academy of Sciences is continuing its methodical research into these urban and rural dwelling-places; they have revealed some original features of the local culture, notably the curious religious cult of the "Danubian horsemen".

To an even greater extent than the Pannonians, the Illyrians took the destiny of the Empire in hand when it seemed most seriously threatened. Under the influence of Rome, these uncouth Indo-European peoples—whose language is still preserved in Albania—revealed not only military talent but a political ability that would enable two of them—Diocletian and Constantine—to set the whole Mediterranean world on a new path. The memory of Diocletian has been kept alive by the town of Split (Italian: Spalato), which contains the vast palace—a combination of the austere and the sumptuous—built by the Soldier Emperor for his retirement. An account of it was published more than fifty years ago by two French arch-aeologists, J. Zeiller and A. Hébrard; but this building—the finest demonstration of the transition between the civilization of Rome and that of the Middle Ages—still continues to arouse interest. More recently, another Dalmatian site, Salone—which is rich in early Christian remains—inspired a major work by E. Dyggve, the great Danish historian of the civil and religious architecture of this transitional period. The work of these foreign scholars in no way detracts from the very real achievement of Yugoslav archaeologists in the period since their country gained its independence; since the Second World War, excavations in Yugoslavia—as in all the People's Republics—have been particularly encouraged by the authorities.

Rumania—which, whatever the political vicissitudes it has undergone, has never forgotten the Latin origins of its culture—has understandably made a special effort in the field of Roman archaeology. The finds have been exceptionally important, the most notable being the Trophy of Adamklissi *(Plate 77)*, which bears witness to the event that gave birth to the nation: the conquest of Dacia by Trajan in the early years of the 2nd century A.D. It consists of a huge rotunda set in the middle of the Dobruja steppes, with crude sculptures illustrating episodes in the war—a constrast to the finished art with which the same events are commemorated on Trajan's Column in Rome. The work of local craftsmen, these sculptures were in the past judged unworthy of the art of Rome at its peak. At the beginning of the present century, they gave rise to bitter disputes among archaeologists, some of whom thought that they belonged to the 1st century B.C., while others placed them in the 4th century A.D. On one point, however, they were all agreed—that the sculptures themselves were appalling. Today we look upon them with a different eye, finding in their stylized geometrical forms a power of expression akin to that of much contemporary art. Since the Second World War, the Rumanian People's Republic has made a study of this noteworthy monument of the nation's past, in which the most precise techniques of architectural research, geology, and ethnology have been employed in the interests of historical accuracy.

75,76

PROBLEMS AND METHODS
OF ROMAN ARCHAEOLOGY

II

General working conditions

In our brief summary of the history of Roman archaeology, we have made a rapid survey of the main excavations. We shall now turn to the methods employed.

As we have shown, the first aim of Roman archaeology is to bring large-scale buildings and sometimes even whole towns to light. It is thus mainly concerned with architecture and the history of town-planning. The excavation methods consequently cannot be quite the same as those employed on prehistoric sites, where the principal aim is to recover small and fragile objects from the soil. This does not mean the use of rough and ready methods that would destroy everything except walls or particularly resistant objects, such as stone carvings and mosaics. The first difficulty encountered in setting out to explore a Roman site is that of reconciling the massive scale of the operations with the need for preserving the most fragile remains and disturbing the order of the most resistant objects as little as possible. Obviously it is impossible to excavate a whole town with the aid of a trowel and a brush; but there are cases in which such tools must be used to the exclusion of all others, and the person in charge must be constantly on the alert to see when a change of method is needed.

Rescue operations

It would be hypocritical not to recognize that the work often has to be carried out in conditions that are far from perfect. It must always be remembered that Roman ruins cover a considerable area and are only in a good state of preservation when they are buried deeply under the surface of the ground, or when they are in out-of-the-way places where human habitation has long ceased. As a result of technical progress and population spread, more and more sites are coming to light. In one way this is a good thing, but it must not be forgotten that the immediate result of an archaeological find is to deprive the site concerned of the protection afforded to it by nature. Those in charge of archaeological services have no right to ignore any chance discovery brought to their notice, on the pretext that they have not the equipment with which to follow it up correctly. While it is true that it is better not to excavate at all than to excavate badly, it is better to excavate badly than to leave a site at the mercy of incompetent investigators or, even worse, of plunderers. In theory, the law has bestowed exceptional powers on the authorities responsible for the preservation of ancient monuments; in most countries, they have the right to stop any work that might result in the destruction of a ruin or any removal of the objects it may contain. But let us have no illusions on this point: whenever vested interests are at stake, some way is found of getting round the law, even if it is not openly violated. When the workmen preparing the site for a hospital, a school, a block of flats, a factory, or a road come across ancient remains, public opinion—often aroused by the builders, for whom any stoppage in the work, be it only for a few days, represents an enormous loss—is quick to side against the guardians of the past. Until quite recently, the press took great pleasure in depicting them as old fogies, as decrepit as the ruins they sought to preserve. The present vogue for archaeology has, however, done something to modify this attitude, if it has achieved nothing else. Nevertheless nearly everywhere Roman remains are undergoing the same fate as the Baths of Paris, which were sacrified in 1935 to make way for the new buildings of the Collège de France. In a number of large cities, unscrupulous contractors keep quiet about the finds made in the foundations of the buildings they are putting up. Only a few years ago, the extraordinary catacombs of the Via Latina in Rome escaped destruction only because an employee who had been sacked by the firm responsible for the work warned the authorities. In the rural areas, the modern practice of deep ploughing will almost certainly destroy many remains long preserved in the soil. In such cases, the head of the archaeological services—if there is one—obviously has the duty to carry out a rescue operation, though he often does not have the means to do so. The difficulties vary according to the region: in the under-developed countries, where ancient ruins are particularly numerous, archaeologists are often obliged, for social reasons, to employ a vast army of workers; the problem then is one of logistics. In Europe, on the other hand, labour is scarce and expensive, and it is often necessary to use voluntary teams. However well-intentioned they may be, such workers lack experience and may often be able to spend only short periods on the job. Again, they raise problems of board and lodging. The main problem everywhere is that of recruiting skilled workers, whose level of education does not matter as long as they possess "archaeological flair". Quite often, almost illiterate workmen will sense at once what part of an apparently vacant site conceals a ruin, while scientists with long years of study behind them may go on prospecting in vain.

Archaeology in unusual conditions

The way of carrying out an excavation and the difficulties and problems encountered will naturally vary a great deal according to the conditions in which the remains have been preserved. Every excavation has its story, and we obviously cannot relate them all here. The most interesting Gallo-Roman discoveries in France over the past few years, particularly at Arles, but also at Bavay, at Reims, and more recently at Bourges, have consisted of galleries that, even originally, were underground, or of buildings buried beneath a modern city. It requires little effort of imagination to realize how different the obstacles encountered in such work are from those occurring on sites that have been abandoned by man for centuries and are covered only with earth and vegetation, the density of the latter varying according to the climate.

Everybody has heard about underwater archaeology, whose first great achievement was the exploration, just before World War I, of a Roman ship sunk off the Tunisian coast about 80 B.C. with a full cargo of Greek objects of art for the dwellings of the Roman aristocracy. This technique has been greatly improved since then with the invention of the independent diving-suit, which enables archaeologists to visit underwater sites for themselves. It has proved extremely effective, not only in recovering works of art, but in studying the architecture of ancient ports, shipbuilding techniques, and the composition of cargoes. These are questions of capital importance for the economic history of the ancient world, which is now, with good reason, one of the main concerns of the archaeologist. However, the procedure for exploring a Roman wreck is no different from that used for any sunken vessel, whatever its age.

For a long time, the exploration of necropoles—also very important for the study of economic history—was mistakenly considered as work that could be entrusted to amateurs. In fact, it requires methods very similar to those employed on prehistoric sites; not only must the smallest potsherd be carefully collected, but the ground must be "squared" to make it possible to mark the exact position occupied by each object in the tomb. If we hurry over these aspects of research, it is not because they are lacking in interest, but because they follow rules that apply to all branches of archaeology. On the other hand, the exploration of a whole urban site is an undertaking mainly confined to Roman archaeology, and demands from the archaeologist not only a general technical competence but also a complete familiarity with the whole of Latin studies.

Excavation of a town: identification of the site

First of all, the site must be identified; this task is rendered easier by the existence of ancient maps. The two most important—the Table of Peutinger and the Itinerary of Antoninus—are medieval copies of a map of the Empire made in the 3rd century A.D. The original was more in the nature of a guide to travellers, showing little concern for overall geographical accuracy, but meticulously recording the roads and the distances between halts.

Except where the figures have been inaccurately transcribed—and such mistakes are unfortunately frequent—these documents permit us to determine the sites of the Roman towns, provided the general lie of the roads is known and some of the halts can be identified. The roads themselves can be redis-covered by means of traces of the paving and of the statues and buildings (usually tombs) that bordered them. An even better way is to follow the milestones (a Roman mile was 1650 yards)—in Gaul, these occur at intervals of a league instead of a mile. At the beginning of the present century, Com-mandant Donau, a survey officer in southern Tunisia, trained his horse to stop automatically every 1650 yards and in this way discovered a great many Roman milestones. Today it is simpler to discover them from the air. Many of the towns have kept their ancient names in more or less altered form. Here epigraphy can offer confirmation, since on nearly every site at least one stone inscribed with the Latin name of the town comes to light.

Modern techniques help to trace less important sites such as isolated villas and military posts. As already mentioned, Roman archaeology has often made use of aerial photography to find frontier posts isolated in the desert of Africa or Syria.

In every region, photographs taken from aircraft have been particularly effective in revealing traces of ancient divisions of land, as in Tunis, where the Romans divided at least half the territory into regular squares of 124 acres each, for survey purposes. These show up astonishingly well on photographs, if they are taken in a favourable light. Aerial photography also reveals traces of land development—terraces, dams, canals, and even plantations, which show as regular scars on the ground. It also reveals the lay-out of the towns, permitting the excavators to set to work at once on the most important sectors of an untouched site.

Tracing monuments

C. Courtois, the historian of the Vandals, once remarked teasingly that archaeologists always call the biggest ruin on an unknown site "the baths".

He was, in fact, quite right, for the baths were always the largest building in a Roman community, like the church in a mediaeval village or the school in a modern one. They occurred everywhere, in the smallest hamlets and on private estates. The ceilings were always vaulted, no woodwork being used because of the danger of fire. They were fashioned from huge blocks of stone, bound with the famous Roman cement and having the resistance of the hardest rock. They have often remained intact, transformed into underground passages by the accumulation of the soil above them. The keystone of one of these vaults has sometimes been shattered, but the fragments lying on the ground have proved practically indestructible. The presence of such fragments is a sure indication of the existence of an ancient site. The first task of the excavator who discovers them is to collect potsherds from the surface of the site.

Importance of pottery

Pottery provides invaluable clues for the "detective of the past". The ancient Mediterranean peoples used baked clay for their utensils, whereas we use not only crockery, but glass (which was not unknown to them, but was then a luxury product), metal, and of course all kinds of plastic. From this clay they fashioned the containers for those liquids most essential to their subsistence: oil and wine. As these were the principal source of trade, the large potteries were always attached to the main commercial centres. The painted vases that spread from Corinth and Athens to all parts of the Mediterranean are well known. Roman pottery is obviously not of the same artistic value, but it is equally useful to the historian, or at least it will be once the different series have been classified with the same care as those of Greece. The best-quality Roman vases are made of a red clay that could achieve the thinness and lightness of metal; they are decorated in relief and often bear the names of the potteries where they were manufactured. These were enormous concerns, and often belonged to high dignitaries. It has been possible to locate the different potteries and follow their history: from the 3rd to the 1st century B.C., the Campanians dominated the market; then for a brief period —from 30 B.C. to about 30 A.D.—the monopoly passed into the hands of the Etrurians of Arezzo *(Plate 135)*, whose coral-red goblets (as delicate as eggshells) and elegantly decorated lamps were sold throughout the Empire and even as far afield as India, where a large store of them has been found a few miles south of Pondicherry. Then, from the 1st century A.D., the lead was taken by the Gallic potteries in the Rouergue, and a little later on in Auvergne. In time, the main centres shifted to more outlying areas, notably the Argonne and the Rhineland, while others prospered in Spain and North Africa *(Plate 131)*, where a light sigillated pottery was launched.

Thus a broken fragment of a kitchen utensil can be of the utmost value for dating a site. Only coins are more useful, since they are marked with the year in which they were issued; but they are found less frequently, whereas pottery is always present. A collection of potsherds from the surface enables the archaeologist to gain an approximate idea, at the outset, of the period of occupation of the site he is prospecting. Later on, the fragments collected from the soil itself will guide the course of the excavation at every stage.

Tactics of excavation

How should an excavation be started? It would not be practicable to start digging round the huge fragments of masonry from the baths that first drew attention to the site; if they have collapsed it will be necessary to move them, or break them up, so as to avoid the risk of being buried beneath them. It is better to go a bit farther on and try to trace the course of a wall at the surface of the soil. The excavator will be in luck if the finds ends of pillars projecting from the ground near the wall; he may then have an opportunity of starting his excavation with a relatively imposing and well-preserved building. It is true that certain modern excavators have a somewhat Puritan attitude and are inclined to consider the unearthing of a fine building as a rather frivolous aim. But archaeology need not involve a complete repudiation of all aesthetic feeling.

Finding the original ground-level

Let us go back to our wall, near which we have observed a few truncated, but upright, pillars. The problem now is to find the original ground-level. We have already indicated that, for archaeological remains to be in a good state of preservation, the layer of protective earth must be of a certain depth —on the average about 6 feet. We must now carefully excavate the wall and the columns down to their bases. If all goes well, we shall find that they are set on firm foundations and that there is a solid layer at floor-level— perhaps a pavement of flagstones or mosaics. Even if we find only a floor of beaten earth, we must resist the temptation to go on to see what lies beneath, for in this case we have probably chanced on a mediaeval building, which may be of considerable interest and must not be destroyed—even if there is a more ancient level below—until it has been completely studied and recorded. In every case, the preliminary soundings must be carried out with the utmost care; the area of excavation should be extremely restricted and the digging should be carried out by a small number of experienced workers under the constant supervision of the archaeologist. The latter must collect in boxes all the objects found at the different levels, and must draw cross-sections of the diggings in his notebook, which should also contain photographs of the work. This is essential if some idea is to be gained of what has happened to the building since ancient times. No architectural fragments should be removed until their exact location has been noted, for in most cases the roof will have caved in and they are the only means whereby the upper part of the building can be scientifically reconstructed. If this practice had always been conscientiously followed, we should have been spared a great deal of controversy. To take but one example, one of the thorniest problems of the history of Roman architecture is that of the roofing of the main entrance hall of the palace built by Domitian on the Palatine in the con-

83
84
85
86
→

cluding years of the 1st century A.D. Some think that this *aula regia*, measuring about 130 by 115 feet, was an open courtyard; others think it had a wooden roof; and yet others that it was covered with stone vaulting.

The advocates of the last opinion—which is probably the correct one—point out that the first excavators found fragments of masonry lying on the ground and that these could only have come from a vault; unfortunately, these fragments were not studied and recorded with sufficient care to convince the incredulous. Precautions must be redoubled if there is reason to think that fragments of the upper part of the building in fragile materials, such as wood, may have been preserved, though this happens only in certain exceptional cases; we have already briefly described the precautions that enabled V. Spinazzola to save the balconies and roofs of the houses on the Via dell' Abbondanza in Pompeii.

Reconstructing the town plan

Once the ancient ground-level has been reached, the excavation takes a new direction. In the case of a town, the best method, in our opinion, is first to trace the network of streets. Sometimes we may light upon one of them straight away, particularly if an aerial photograph has been used in deciding on the first sounding. Quite often, a triumphal arch—usually an extremely resilient structure—has remained intact above the ancient level; there is every likelihood that it spans an important road, particularly if it has been erected as the gateway to the town or the approach to a square. If the first sounding happens to be on the inside of a building, it is advisable —even before the building has been completely cleared—to try to find the way out to the street; the lie of the street can than be ascertained and it can be followed until the intersecting streets are found. It will then be possible to ascertain whether the town was built according to a regular plan as were most Roman towns, except for a few minor ones built on uneven terrain, such as Thugga (Dugga) in north-west Tunisia *(Plates 63, 64)*. Once the lay-out has been determined and checked by a series of soundings (for example, at the points where crossroads may be expected), if will be possible to establish a rational plan of operations, spread over several sectors.

All this work should be carried out with the precautions already mentioned. In particular, the temptation to go below the ancient ground-level should be avoided like the plague. This level is the one that corresponds to the last regular occupation of the site. In the case of a town destroyed by war or natural disaster, it will be the one immediately preceding the catastrophe. Amateur excavators often cause a great deal of damage because of their unfortunate propensity for exploring "underground passages"—which are often only cisterns or drains and not the repositories of hidden treasure they are fondly imagined to be. Even when it is obvious that a paving or even a floor of beaten earth is of a very late period, it must never be destroyed in the first phase of the excavation. Once a rough plan of the town has been established, the buildings may be explored; the order in which they will be tackled is generally determined by practical considerations and varies according to the circumstances. Certain relatively well-preserved buildings are shored up by the earth and debris they contain; they can be excavated only when the upper parts have been consolidated. The sites of others may be occupied by modern buildings, whose inhabitants will have to be rehoused. Finally, there is the problem of disposing of the earth dislodged by the excavation; this is common to every type of digging and its importance naturally varies according to the extent of the area explored.

Preserving archaeological remains

When the first phase of the excavation is completed the question of preserving the finds arises. In Roman archaeology, special attention must be paid to the frescoes and mosaics; these are typically Roman art-forms, and they are liable to be found in most excavations of any size. They are extremely fragile and, difficult to transport, and their removal irreparably blemishes the buildings in which they are found. The old solution of transfer to a museum should therefore not be adopted unless there is no other alternative, e.g., when it is impossible to preserve the building. In such cases, the help of extremely skilled and careful technicians is required. One of the greatest services rendered to science by La Blanchère and Gauckler, the first Directors of the Tunisian Department of Antiquities, was to form a team of mosaic-workers at the Museum of Bardo. For a long time, there was no equivalent of this team, except in Italy, and it is thanks to their work and to its own rich past that Tunisia now has the finest collection of Roman pavements in the world *(Plates 105–111)*. In preparing a painting or a mosaic for transport, it is unwise to trust to the solidity of the underlying layer of plaster or cement. The same procedure must be used as for changing the canvas of a painting: first of all, a piece of material must be pasted on to the front surface, then the backing must be removed with meticulous care, and finally a new backing must be prepared and the painting or mosaic affixed to it. This infinitely delicate work must be carried out even when the paintings or pavements are not going to be removed from the building; when they are set back in place after being thus consolidated, care must be taken to see that they are protected from their greatest enemy —humidity. It is because this precaution was neglected that the frescoes of the House of Augustus on the Palatine have almost disappeared, even though the Restoration Institute in Rome—probably the best in the world—recently did its utmost to save them. The paintings have a second enemy—light. It is not enough to cover them with a protective coating, and it is of course out of the question to repaint them (though this unfortunate expedient was still being resorted to, not so long ago). The problem has been solved by the chemists, who have found ways of making the colours fast. Mosaics are naturally more resistant, except when they are made of glass paste; however, until the end of the 2nd century A.D., this material was not generally used except in mural or ceiling mosaics. Marble mosaics can be vigorously sandpapered to restore their colour, and to keep a pavement intact all that is needed is to protect the cement that binds it from damp and from variations in temperature. In severe winters, it should be covered with a layer of sand.

Dating buildings by inscriptions

The next step is to identify and date the buildings, and reconstitute their history. Sometimes identification and dating are helped by the discovery of an inscription, and such discoveries are fortunately quite common. Most of the public buildings were erected by magistrates, who covered all the expenses in order to increase their social prestige. They naturally wanted their generosity to receive the maximum publicity, and so they had a prominent inscription placed on each building, indicating its purpose, the name and title of the donor, and the amount spent on inaugural ceremonies. When such an inscription is discovered, the only problem—if it is intact—is to decide whether it was an integral part of the original building or whether it was incorporated in it during rebuilding. In North Africa, the Byzantines hastily put up an enormous network of forts in the provinces they had just captured from the Vandals, using a great deal of material from earlier buildings, particularly stones with inscriptions, since these were in better shape than the others. Thus it is always important to find the place occupied by the inscription in the architecture of the building. To fill in gaps in the inscription is the business of the epigraphist; this is usually possible, since the precision of the formulae employed by the ancients is equalled only by the skill with which the moderns have classified them. Unfortunately there is often some uncertainty about the date, for, except in a few provinces and towns, the ancient Romans did not follow any uniform chronological system. The most specific clue is found in the Emperor's titles in the frequent cases when the building is dedicated to him: the number of years of his reign is given by the "tribunician power", which was regularly renewed on the 10th December every year.

Stratigraphy

When there is no dedication, as in the case of a private house, the building can be dated by stratigraphy or by a study of the building methods employed. Soundings in the ancient ground-level, which can be cautiously explored at this point, will yield material that can in general be taken as dating from before the time of building, though quite often even fairly bulky objects of a later date may have invaded the subsoil. Those objects that can be dated with precision—particularly coins and potsherds—enable us to determine the *terminus post quem*, i.e., the period preceding the erection of the building. It may happen that the *terminus* is much earlier than the buildings, since the foundations may have displaced quite a depth of soil. These soundings are also of value in revealing the possible existence of even older buildings, which may belong to a pre-Roman civilization; they should be continued down to virgin soil in order to determine the original configuration of the site, which may have been modified in the course of the building operations.

Building methods

Dating on the basis of the building methods employed is a reliable procedure, provided that the history of these methods has been carefully studied beforehand. It must be remembered that they vary considerably according to the region. G. Lugli's monumental history of Roman building techniques in Italy offers extremely precise criteria: for example, round about the beginning of the Christian era, masons were in the habit of decorating walls with pebbles set in diagonal criss-cross lines, and the presence of a "reticulated" wall shows definitely that the building dates from the beginning of the Empire. Bricks were increasingly employed in the Imperial era, sometimes singly, sometimes in layers cutting the masonry; they are often stamped with the name of the brickworks where they were made and with the date of manufacture. A study of the markings on the bricks of the Pantheon in Rome, for example, proved that it had been entirely rebuilt by Hadrian, even though the dedication is in the name of Agrippa, the son-in-law of Augustus. Architectural developments also afford a means of dating: for example, the groined vault formed by the intersection of two semi-cylindrical cradle vaults made its appearance during the 1st century A.D. and came into general use towards the end of that century. Finally, the methodical study of sculptured, painted, or mosaic decorations is also helpful in ascertaining the date of a building, provided of course that they are contemporary with the building and not later additions. With all these aids to dating, the Roman archaeologist need rarely have recourse to the methods evolved by modern physics, which are in general much less precise than those afforded by a thorough knowledge of his own field. Nevertheless, dating by the carbon-14 method or by geomagnetic measurement can be of service in certain very exceptional cases.

The decoration

While the construction date of a building rarely raises any problem that the conscientious archaeologist cannot solve, the dates of subsequent transformations are much more difficult to establish. The refurbishing of wall facings and floors is relatively easy to detect, since traces of the original decoration often survive. In other cases, the archaeologist must rely on the style of the decoration: when a building whose walls date from the 1st century A.D. contains paintings or mosaics that cannot go back any earlier than the 2nd century, it has obviously undergone alterations.

Classification of Roman paintings (Plates 82-89)

The classification of Pompeian mural paintings established by the German scholar, Mau, at the end of the 19th century has proved valid for the whole of the Roman world and has on the whole stood up to criticism. The 2nd century B.C. and the early years of the 1st century B.C. witnessed the first style, which came from the eastern basin of the Mediterranean; with the aid of painted stucco, the decorators of this period tried to reproduce the texture of precious marble. A major change occured about 80 B.C., when walls began to be decorated with *trompe-l'œil* paintings of marble colonnades opening on to mysterious vistas that seemed to stretch to infinity. This second style continued into the Christian era with ever-increasing complications and refinements. This kind of fantasy did not, however, appeal to everybody: the architect Vitruvius, writing between 30 and 20 B.C., made a virulent attack on it—an attack that is a remarkable example of the reaction of the classical spirit against the baroque. Shortly afterwards the third style appeared; in contrast to the illusionism and "surrealism" of the second, it brought back the "closed" wall, dividing it into regular panels. There has been much disagreement about the third style: such leading experts as Ippel and Curtius see it simply as a special tendency that developed parallel with the second style, rather then something succeeding it. Here we must give an example of the traps into which even the most experienced archaeologists may fall. On the Palatine, beneath the Palace of the Flavians built by Domitian about A.D. 90, there is a group of earlier buildings which were left intact when the palace was put up. One of them is decorated with paintings in the second style, mainly on themes borrowed from Egyptian art: they show not only Nilotic landscapes, but also various aspects of the cult of Isis with animal-headed gods and figures dressed like Pharoahs. Now, it is known that Caligula, the second successor of Augustus, was particularly devoted to the cult of Isis—unlike his predecessors, who had persecuted the priests of this religion—and that he had built a chapel dedicated to Isis in his palace. F. Cumont, the great Belgian historian of the religions of the Roman Empire, and G.E. Rizzo, one of the best Italian archaeologists of the early 20th century, were accordingly persuaded that the *aula isiaca*, as the mysterious room beneath the Palace of the Flavians was called, must be the Chapel of Caligula described by Suetonius. It was believed that Claudius took refuge in this room, following the assassination of his nephew Caligula, and that he was found there by the praetorians, who brought him out, trembling, to make him Emperor. G. Lugli, the great historian of Roman architecture, also supported this conclusion, which seemed to give definite evidence of the co-existence of the second and the third styles of Roman paintings, since Caligula reigned from 38 to 42 A.D. Unfortunately, the attribution of the so-called *aula isiaca* to Caligula has now been definitely disproved by modern experts on Pompeian paintings, notably the Dutch scholar H. Beyen. The so-called chapel is now seen to be an ordinary room decorated about 20 B.C. in an Egyptian style that was then all the rage as a result of the annexation of Cleopatra's kingdom and the fascination of the Roman nobility with the exotic aspects of the East. The third style continued into Nero's reign, but this romantic ruler, who had a passion for art and was half-mad into the bargain, brought back all the wild, dreamlike fantasy that had been suppressed by the sober Augustus. During his reign, extravagant and sumptuous mural paintings proliferated; they were inspired mainly by the theatre, to which the Emperor was so devoted that he could barely distinguish between the fictional world of the drama and that of real life. The magnificent palace that he built on the ruins of Rome after the fire, with its lakes, forests, imaginary towns, and ingenious illusion-producing devices was nothing more than a vast stage setting. The spread of this fourth style shows that, contrary to what the historians of the Senatorial party have written, Nero has a profound influence over his subjects and that, in the aesthetic field at least, the great majority of them did not hesitate to follow him.

Mosaics (Plates 90-127)

From the time of the destruction of Pompeii, the history of Roman painting becomes increasingly obscure, since the evidence is largely lacking. However, at this point, another decorative art came to the fore: the mosaic. The first mosaics were Greek and date back to the 5th century B.C. At that time they were made of unpolished pebbles, but in the Hellenistic period the mosaic was raised to the level of a luxury art—for example, the mosaics of the Casa del Fauno in Pompeii, including the famous Alexander's Battle. Finally, the

93

94

95

103

104

109 →

110 →

POLYS TEFANVS RATIONIS EST ARCHEVS

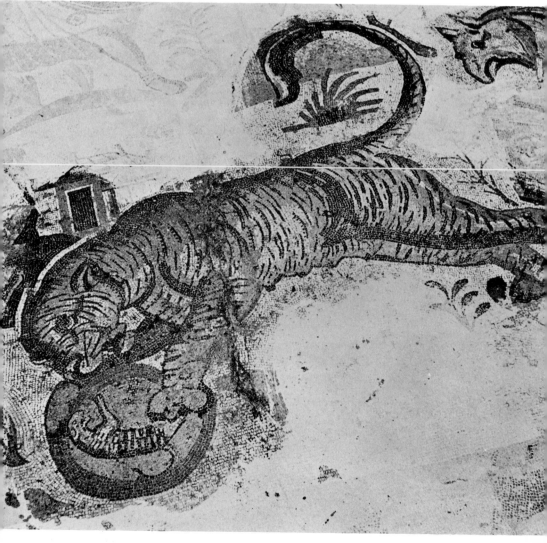

121
122
123
124 →

125

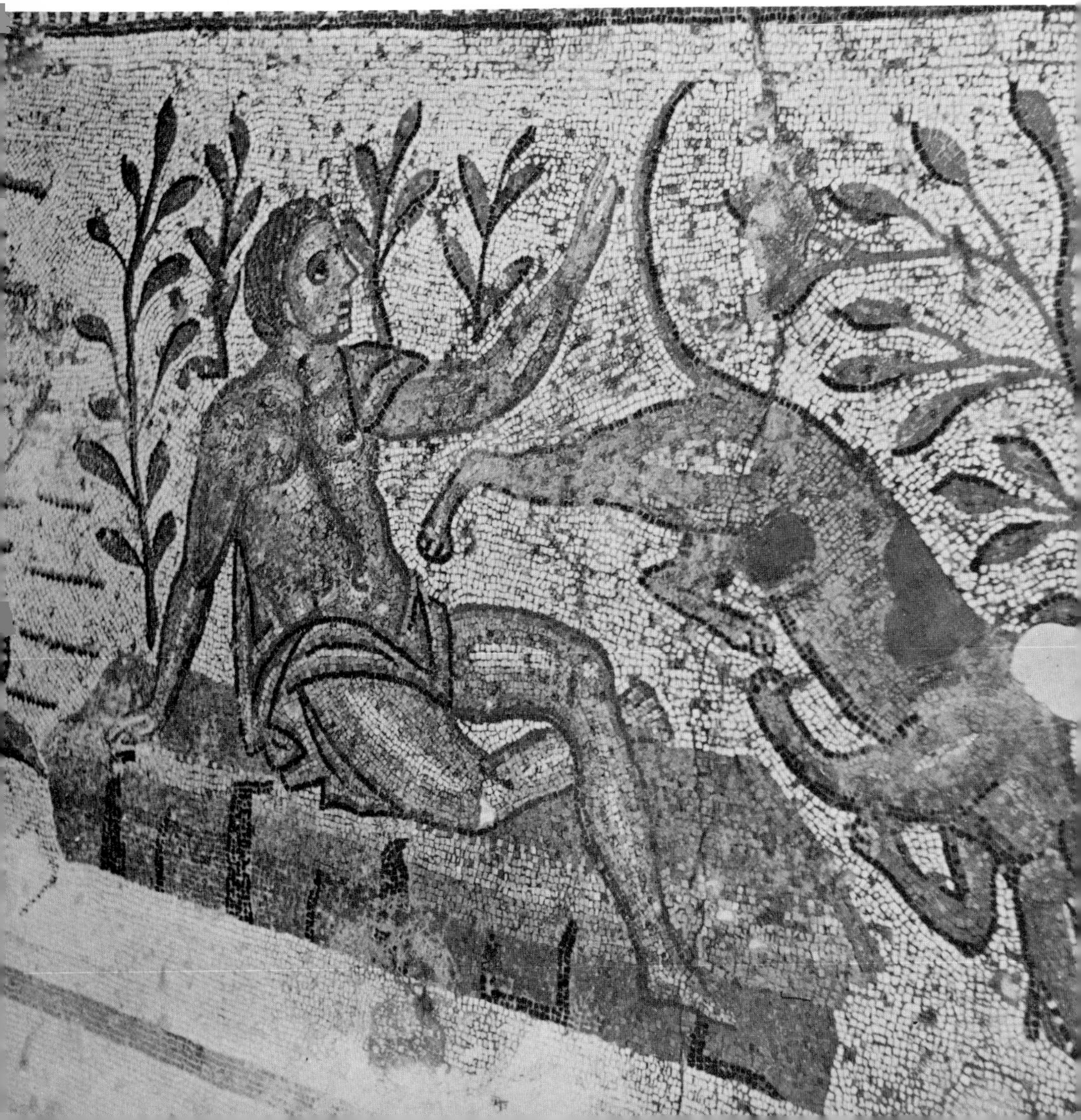

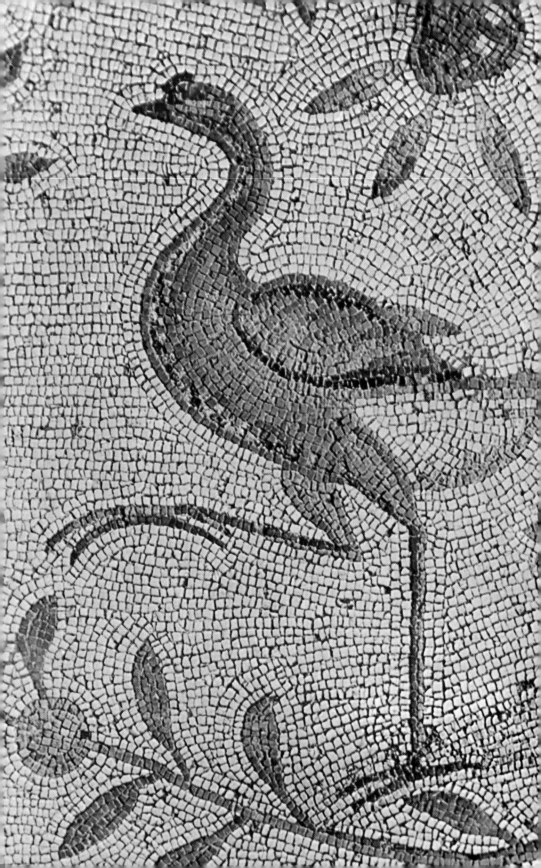

Romans made it a widespread and more commonplace mode of decoration. Until the end of the 1st century A.D., the Roman floor mosaic, or *tesselatum*, consisted exclusively of simple geometrical patterns in black on a white background. From the 2nd century on, there was a greater variety of patterns and in particular of schools: while the Italian workshops used black and white for patterns that were often based on plant forms, animals, and human figures, those in North Africa treated similar subjects in colour. The mosaics of Syria, also in colour, were put together on more classical principles than those of Africa. The chronology of this art raises a number of difficulties and has been the cause of much lively controversy—for example, the dispute over the dating of the mosaics of Piazza Armerina. Following a meeting held in Paris in 1963, international co-operation in this field has now been established and it is hoped that it will be possible to agree on a general Corpus, such as already exists for pottery, but not yet for mural painting, and only very partially for sculpture.

Identification of buildings

The identification of buildings is facilitated by the standardized nature of Roman town planning. Every town sought to have those buildings that were indispensable to the Roman way of life, and they were often built with the help of architects from Rome itself. Thus, a large number of towns in Gaul or Britain—for example, Paris, Alesia, Saint-Bertrand-de-Comminges, Colchester, St Albans, and Lincoln—had the same type of *forum*, in the form of a large rectangle bordered with shops and porticos, with a temple at one end, while at the other stood the *basilica*, which served as a courthouse, and the *curia*, where the town council met. Two or three types of baths, varying in size according to the resources of the inhabitants (the largest followed the lay-out of the Baths of Titus and Trajan in Rome), and two or three types of theatre occur from one end of the Empire to the other. A number of the amphitheatres are models of the Coliseum on a more or less reduced scale *(Plates 29, 30)*.

Yet this uniformity, which could be monotonous, is much less apparent when the details of the buildings are examined. Thus, in Africa, there are at least two kinds of public squares, one predominantly administrative in function, as in Timgad *(Plates 50–55)*, while the other is so surrounded by temples and chapels that it is more like the courtyard of a temple and seems to anticipate the enclosure of the mosque. The space given at the baths to the heated rooms in relation to the *frigidarium* varies according to the climate but the *natatio* was nearly always on a large scale. Some theatres have the seats ranged in a semi-circle on a hillside, as what the custom in Greece; others, following Pompey's example at Rome, are built on flat ground and their hemicycles are usually supported by several tiers of vaulted radiating galleries. A building intermediate between a theatre and an amphiteatre is often found in Gaul and sometimes in the Balkans. The ingenuity of the architects in providing buildings suitable for the various religious cults prevailing in the Empire is particularly noteworthy. Both western and eastern gods—Mithras, the Syrian Baals, the Great Mother of the Gods from Anatolia, Isis and the other Egyptian gods, the old Celtic divinities and those bequeathed by Carthage to Africa and Sardinia—were housed in buildings adapted to the needs of each rite, yet laid out in rational fashion and decorated in classical style. For example, the Gallo-Roman temple consisted of a square *cella* surrounded by a porticoed courtyard, while the statues of the African temple were kept in three *cellae* opening off the end of the courtyard. After the reconciliation between Christianity and the Empire, the builders had to meet the needs of the new religion, whose adherents had until then been meeting more or less secretly, often—like other mystic sects— in private houses that were sometimes transformed for the purpose. It seems to have been on Constantine's own initiative that the basilica, a form of building created in Rome in the 2nd century B.C., was adapted to Christian requirements. After various transformations, the basilica had become, in the course of time, particularly suitable for those spectacular gatherings and complicated ceremonials by which the Empire established its psychological domination over the masses. It should also be noted that, in the 1st century

B.C., certain temples of the official religions—for example, those of Venus Genetrix and Mars Ultor, built by Julius Caesar and Augustus respectively— were laid out like basilicas on the inside.

The problem of ruined buildings
Fire layers and treasure

One of the most important problems for the archaeologist is that of determining the date when buildings were destroyed. Destructions due to violence were generally the result of historical events of the first importance, such as wars and revolutions, but these have not always been recorded with sufficient precision by the ancient historians. For example, a large number of excavations for public works or on building sites at various points of the city of Strasbourg revealed a layer of ashes, whose stratigraphic position and contents showed that it dated from the concluding years of the 1st century A.D. By relating this finding to some rather vague literary and epigraphical evidence, J. J. Hatt was able to prove that in 97 A.D. the XXIst Legion, which guarded the Germanic frontier, mutinied with the support of some of the Suevian Teutons. The rebels, moving to the interior of Gaul, clashed with the loyal VIIIth Legion before Strasbourg. The town and the camp were destroyed in the battle. Trajan, who was then in command at Mainz, crushed the rebellion and dissolved the XXIst Legion, whose name ceased to appear on inscriptions after that date. Archaeology has thus shed light on events that were almost completely ignored by contemporary writers. In another case, archaeology has succeeded in confirming ancient accounts whose accuracy had been wrongly questioned. The Catholic writers accused the Vandals of having systematically destroyed the principal buildings of Carthage, but the late C. Courtois, the historian of the Germanic domination in Africa, considered these accusations ill-founded. However, at the ground level of the largest baths in Carthage—the Baths of Antoninus *(Plate 56)*—a layer of ashes was discovered. It contained an earthenware pot filled with coins, the most recent of which dated from 425 A.D. As Gaiseric took Carthage in 439 A.D., he was obviously responsible for the destruction of the building. Money "treasures", buried by unfortunate people anxious to preserve their wealth in time of trouble, are historical evidence of the first order. A. Blanchet, the great numismatist, has drawn up a list of treasures of this kind found in Gaul; with its aid, it is possible to follow the progress of the invasions that ravaged the country from the middle of the 3rd century.

The painstaking and scholarly study of a treasure of silverware found at Tenes in Algeria enabled J. Heurgon to reconstitute the history, over several generations, or a noble Gallic family that came to Rome with Constantine and was raised to high rank, but fled the city on the approach of the Visigoths, taking refuge in Africa, where it gradually died out in arrogant poverty. Another unexpected discovery recalls the horror of an assassination at court. Emptying the outlet of the latrines at Carthage, we found a fine, though mutilated, marble bust of the Emperor Geta, who was strangled in his mother's arms in 212 A.D. by his brother Caracalla. The victim was declared a State criminal, and the Carthiginians sought to curry favour with the authorities by defiling his images is this way.

Interpretation of figures on monuments

The third and last part of the archaeologist's task is the most complicated of all. It consists, once monuments and buildings have been found, identified, and dated, in trying to ascertain the meaning the ancients gave to them. So far, we have dealt mainly with buildings. We must now turn to sculptures and paintings, not only to determine the time at which they were created, but to discover their meaning and aesthetic value. This task will take us to the frontier between archaeology and the history of art—branches of scholarship that are distinct, but sometimes difficult to separate.

Portraits (Plates 141-154)

Unlike the Greeks who at a very early date—at any rate, from the 5th century onwards—considered that the essential, if not the only, aim of artistic creation was the pursuit and achievement of beauty, the Romans always saw art as one technique, among many others, to be put at the service of those social and political ideals they considered to be the supreme goal of mankind. Thus they considered the portrait—one of the first art forms they developed—to be a psychological tool by means of which politicians and the heads of noble families could assert their authority and bear witness to their own glory and that of their ancestors. Roman statues, as H. Kähler has convincingly demonstrated, were rarely conceived as things in themselves like those of the Greeks. Most often they were placed in an architectural setting that adds to their effect—for example, the large statue of an Emperor (whose restoration as a statue of Augustus is inaccurate, since it dates from the 2nd century A.D.) that occupies the central niche on the stage of the theatre at Orange. For the same reason, the Roman portraitist was chiefly concerned with emphasizing the personality of his model, bringing out such public qualities as energy and courage, whereas the Greek artist either took him as a universal type and idealized him, or—in the so-called "physiognomical" portrait—sought to express his emotional attributes. The period in which Rome completed its conquest of the world—the 2nd and 1st centuries B.C.—has left us a series of works that are generally qualified as realist but which it would be more accurate to call expressionist. In a recent work, the American scholar R. Brilliant has shown that the essential aim of these pictures was to show the social standing of the subject, in particular by means of gesture. From the establishment of the empire, the first aim of the portrait was to spread the sovereign's image, in which lay part of his supernatural power. Private individuals showed their loyalty by imitating the chief, guide, and model placed by Providence at the head of mankind. From the aesthetic point of view, three trends may be discerned from the 1st to the 4th century, each predominating in turn according to the period. The classical trend prevailed under Augustus, reappeared in the 2nd century under Hadrian, in the 3rd under Gallienus (253–268), and in the first thirty years of the 4th century under Constantine; it corresponds to the humanist ideal of the Roman Empire, its desire to maintain the cultural heritage of Greece. Romantic and baroque trends are to be found in opposition to this ideal in the time of Nero and in the second half of the 2nd century. Finally the expressionist—i.e., the so-called "realist"—tradition of the republican era reappears under Vespasian (70–79) and in the 3rd century produces intensely powerful works that are undoubtedly among the finest Roman portraits. In the period of the Tetrarchy, it even achieves a cubist approach. Iconography is a very special branch of Roman archaeology, and the methods used by experts—among whom may be cited J. Charbonneaux and F. Chamoux in France, W.H. Gross in Germany, H. Jucker in Switzerland, and Mrs Felleti Maj in Italy—have attained a high degree of precision. Sculpture and bronzes can now be dated to within a few years by comparisons with coinage.

Reliefs of Historical scenes

Another specifically Roman form of official monument is the historical relief. In 13 B.C., the Senate dedicated an altar of peace to Augustus on the occasion of the Emperor's return from a tour of inspection of the western provinces. The monument was erected on the Campus Martius beside the Tiber. It was reconstructed close to its original site on the occasion of the bimillenary of Augustus in 1938. The altar is surrounded by a marble enclosure with sculptured reliefs showing the solemn procession at the dedication ceremony—the figures include Augustus himself, members of his family, the priests, and the high officers of State. These majestic friezes hold a place in Roman art similar to that held in Greek art by the friezes of the Parthenon. Since F. von Duhn identified them in 1879—an identification that has been contested only once, unsuccessfully at that—all the historians of Roman art, one after the other, have studied the various historical, iconographical, and aesthetic problems that this notable monument raises in spite of being so well known and clear in its intentions. Among the countless studies in various languages, pride of place must go to the official work by G. Moretti, which appeared in 1948, after its author's death.

Just as Augustus remained a model for all his successors, the Ara Pacis (Altar of Peace) *(Plate 180)* was frequently imitated—first of all by Claudius in the Altar of Piety, the reliefs of which have been incorporated in the façade of the Villa Medici, then by Domitian, Trajan, and Marcus Aurelius. Most of the leading museums—in particular, the Louvre—contain some of these great official works, whose pictorial rather than sculptural nature was well understood nearer our own time by Rubens and Delacroix. Large fragments of these altar-reliefs are still coming to light in Rome; in 1939, for example, during work in the basement of the Apostolic Chancellery on the old Campus Martius, two friezes sculptured on the orders of Domitian were discovered. One shows the arrival in Italy of Domitian's father Vespasian, at the end of the the civil war that followed Nero's death in 68–69; the other shows Domitian himself going off to war, guided by the gods and followed by his army. This discovery, of which an excellent account by F. Magi was published shortly afterwards, has opened up new perspectives on this period of Roman art, which had been studied until then exclusively in terms of the decorations on the Arch of Titus.

At the beginning of the 2nd century, the Empire sought new ways of consolidating its psychological domination of the masses, and the imposing sculptured columns of Trajan *(Plate 192)* and Marcus Aurelius were built. They still tower some 100 feet above modern Rome and are the most perfect symbols of the power of the Caesars. As these vast monuments have survived all the vicissitudes of the Eternal City intact, it has not been necessary to restore them. They nevertheless raise a number of problems, the first being that of their significance: are they triumphal monuments or tombs (the base of Trajan's Column contained the Emperor's ashes)? Then there is the question of artistic influences: so far, all research on this point suggests that they were completely original in conception. Finally, there are the aesthetic problems raised by their enormous spiral friezes, like film-strips in stone, showing the whole history of the wars in the Danube valley, whose almost virgin landscape is admirably expressed in all its savagery. Not the least interesting problem is that of the differences between the two columns. All the figures on Trajan's Column are idealized heroes, whose tribulations do nothing to alter their physical perfection and nobility of spirit. Those on the Column of Marcus Aurelius, however, are tortured in body and embittered in spirit by what they have gone through. In the space of the two generations that separated the conquest of Dacia from the first Teutonic invasion, the Roman Empire had undergone an extremely serious intellectual, aesthetic, and moral crisis anticipating the great spiritual revolution that was shortly to transform Mediterranean man. A monument that has just been brought to light, even though it is a familiar Roman landmark, bears witness to a later phase of the crisis: the Arch of Septimius Severus at the far end of the Forum, beneath the Capitoline Hill. Its reliefs show, extremely effectively, the brutal energy of the Roman Army and its leaders in their merciless fight against the powers threatening the destruction of the Empire.

By his analysis of such works, the archaeologist can perform a valuable service for the historian dealing with the centuries-old problem of the causes of the fall of the Roman Empire. Since Rostovtzeff's great *Social and Economic History of the Roman Empire*, whose appearance in 1926 marked a vital turning-point in Roman studies, most works on the subject have given a great deal of space to the study of monuments: for example, P. Grimal's *Civilisation romaine* and Aymard's *Rome et son Empire*.

Provincial and folk art

The study of monuments and buildings fortunately complements and throws light on the extremely meagre accounts given by ancient historians of the 2nd and 3rd centuries A.D. Furthermore, archaeology is increasingly con-

129

130

SPINARIO

144

145

148

150

151

152

153

154→

155

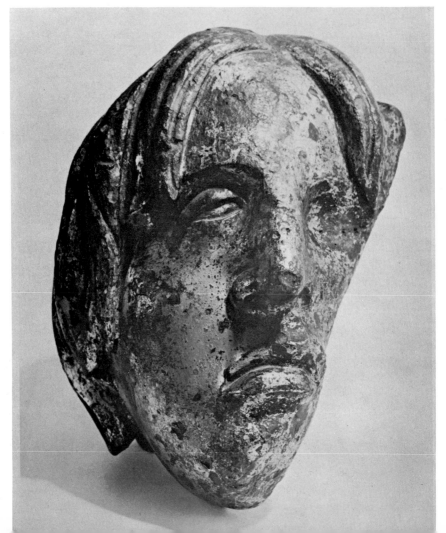

cerned with the political, economic, social, and religious aspects of Roman civilization. It can tell us much about the lower classes of the population, to whom the ancient writers—members of the wealthy classes or employed by them—generally paid scant attention. All parts of the Empire have yielded thousands of art objects made for members of the middle classes, soldiers, artisans, peasants, or slaves. They include decorated tombs, votive offerings to the gods, shop-signs, and the like. These humble works were long despised because of their "barbarous" neglect of the canons of classical art. Today we are interested in both their form and their content for the light they shed on the psychology of the people. They show, for example, that the fundamental principles of Greek art, which made man the measure of all things and presented an image of the universe transposed according to rational rules, were rejected by a large number of the inhabitants of the Empire, particularly in the outlying regions. In their place, we find procedures akin to those of primitive or child artists. Figures are shown full-face, looking directly at the spectator and apparently quite unconcerned about any action in which they may be engaged. The human body is portrayed without any regard for proportion, the significant parts—such as the eyes—being excessively exaggerated. When there are several figures, the most important generally stands alone facing the spectator, and is flanked in heraldic fashion by the others, who are often smaller and seem to act as his assistants. Costumes and jewellery are rendered in the minutest detail. For the background, the artist employed all the objects, animals, and plants that interested him, without bothering whether the spectator would really see them or not. They are distributed, not according to the rules of perspective (of which the artist was ignorant), but so as to create a harmonious whole. In general his aim was not to instruct the spectator and enable him to understand an event, as the classical artist did, but to convey emotion and establish a spiritual communion between the person represented and those for whom the work was intended. The quality of the objects decorated according to these principles varies considerably; some are utterly crude, while others have an aesthetic value at least equivalent to that of a classical work of art.

The problem of Oriental influence
and the genesis of Mediaeval Art

Of particular importance are the temple frescoes of Dura Europos, whose discovery aroused considerable interest in the world of scholarship round about 1930, since they followed the same artistic principles as Byzantine painting and mosaic-work. It was supposed that they derived from an Oriental inspiration, that had been temporarily eclipsed by that of Greece, but was renewed with the spread of the eastern religions as the ancient world entered its final phase.

This theory still has some support today, but it is generally regarded as being over simple. It has been observed that examples of the "primitive" type of art just described were to be found in practically all the outlying regions of the Empire—North Africa, Spain, Gaul, and especially the Danubian provinces—and even in Italy, near Rome itself, e.g., certain frescoes on the façades of houses in Pompeii, and the carved bricks used as shop-signs in Ostia. It has also been observed, in a deeply perceptive work by E. Will, that the style of the paintings at Dura and the sculptures at Palmyra is essentially different from the Oriental styles preceding Alexander's conquest and that they show definite traces of Greek and Roman influences. Neither the Egyptian nor the Mesopotamians depicted figures full-face, and this practice probably originated in Graeco-Roman art.

These problems have aroused the interest of scholars throughout the world, and they formed the subject of the Eighth International Archaeological Congress held in Paris, in September 1963. They are of capital importance in explaining the transition from ancient art to the art of the Middle Ages.

The paintings in the catacombs, to which far too early a date had been assigned in the past (they do not go back any earlier than the end of the 2nd century), are further examples of Roman folk art. It has also been observed that, round about A.D. 170, official art began to be strongly influenced by folk traditions. This is because of the entry into the governing classes of men of lesser birth and education, together with the desire of the authorities to have closer contact with the masses. When Christian art began early in the 4th century, it inherited the "primitive" approach of Roman folk art from several sources. It is not, as was formerly thought, the result of the dislodgement of a Western culture by an Eastern one. Almost all the peoples of the Empire had contributed to it by their radical transformation of the artistic legacy of Greece.

Interpretation of symbols
Funerary symbolism

Research of this kind is extremely helpful in other fields as well. The religious history of the Empire has been completely revised in our own time through the interpretation of the symbols on sculptured monuments; the Belgian scholar, F. Cumont, was largely responsible for this achievement. The archaeologists at the end of the nineteenth and the beginning of the twentieth centuries were wary of this kind of research, which earlier attempts—carried out with more enthusiasm than method—had done much to discredit. Thus the Comte de Clarac, Curator of the Louvre from 1818 to 1847—a very worthy scholar, to whom we are indebted for his publication of a complete illustrated catalogue of the sculpture in his museum—assumed that the S-shaped grooves on certain sarcophagi (called "strigils" after the instruments used by athletes to scrape their bodies clean) symbolized the purification of the soul. As so often happens, scholars then passed from extremes of credulity to extremes of scepticism. The author of the entry "Sarcophagi" in the *Dictionnaire des Antiquités*, an encyclopaedia of the French scholarship of the period, heaped ridicule on the idea that the carvings could have any symbolic meaning, by taking the example of the Dionysiac scenes so frequently found on this type of monument. Surely, he contended, drunken

Satyrs and half-naked Maenads were hardly likely to conjure up thoughts connected with the fear of death and the hope of immortality.

Nevertheless there would be scarcely any point in going to the expense of decorating a sarcophagus or an urn, which would then be buried forever in a tomb, if the decorations had no religious meaning. Cumont's great merit was that of working out a reasonable approach to the interpretation of the symbols on ancient monuments. First of all, we must refuse to give rein to our imagination; the explanation must be furnished by the Ancients themselves, who fortunately took the trouble to hand down the interpretations they gave to the myths and rituals of their religion. Often these interpretations seem extremely far-fetched. When the Greek philosophers started to build up a rational system of metaphysics, they were profoundly shocked by the immorality of most of the legends about the Gods. Incapable of divining the explanations that are today furnished by ethnology, sociology, and psychology, some of them—such as Plato—were content to lay the blame on the poets and banish them from their Republic. But how could Greece give up its Homer? Other philosophers then set out to discover profound symbolic meanings in the myths. It was this approach—first evolved by the Pythagoreans, then accepted by certain Stoics and finally by the Neoplatonists—that inspired the sculptures on the Roman sarcophagi. To take but one example, the Odyssey relates that Aphrodite was captured by her husband Hephaestus in the arms of Ares, her lover, through the device of a net cunningly rigged up round her bed by the craftsman-god; Hephaestus then summoned all the gods to bear witness to his wife's infidelity. This scarcely edifying scene is found on a number of sarcophagi dating from the end of the 2nd century A.D. Does this mean that the persons entombed in them were adepts of Lucian, the Voltaire of the ancient world? Not at all. Cumonti dscovered that some particularly imaginative philosophers considered Aphrodite as a symbol of the soul, Ares as a symbol of the flesh, the net as an image of the need uniting one to the other, and Hephaestus as the demiurge. The word "demiurge", whose literal meaning is "craftsman", was used to designate the maleficent spirit responsible for the degradation of the spirit and its involvement with matter.

Cumont's conclusions, which are contained in two books that are remarkable both for their penetration and their elegance of form, *Le Symbolisme funéraire des Romains* and *Lux Perpetua*, cannot all be unreservedly accepted. He was sometimes led astray by the very brilliance of his erudition, but he undoubtedly laid down the correct procedure for the exegesis of the religious monuments of the Roman Empire. His disciples have achieved some remarkable results: for example, J. Carcopino has used his method to elucidate the meaning of the stucco relief on a hypogeum in the form of a basilica that was discovered near the Porta Maggiore in 1917, showing that the building was used as the secret meeting-place of a Pythagorean sect in the early days of the Empire. H.I. Marrou has demonstrated that the scenes of intellectual life on certains tombs—philosophers teaching, people reading, musicians—symbolize one of the most noble doctrines of the pagan world, namely the "heroification" (a sort of sanctification involving the salvation of the soul) of men and women who have served the intellect and the arts. Under the leadership of F. Matz, who has taken over from J. Rodenwalet, German scholars are engaged on the vast task—started by K. Robert a quarter of a century ago—of assembling all the reliefs from ancient sarcophagi. Their aim is to explain not only their place in the history of ancient art, but also their meaning. They have shown, in particular, that in addition to the philosophy of the period they reflect the official ideology that guided the political activity of the Emperor and the members of the aristocracy.

The symbolism of authority

This ideology is expressed principally in the great monuments of aulic art, of which we have already mentioned the main examples. The studies devoted in recent years to triumphal arches (ranging from the Gate of Rimini, studied by G.A. Manuello, to the Arch of Constantine, interpreted by H. l'Orange and A. von Gerkan, and taking in *inter alia* the arches of Orange and Benevento), to trophies, to the decorated breastplates on a number of imperial statues, to cameos, to silver dishes, etc. show that all these items have symbolic significance: they depict the Emperor not only as a Chief of State and an ever-victorious general, but also as an intermediary between Providence and the world, the possessor of a supernatural good luck that is justified by his virtues and that permits him to triumph over the wicked, obtain peace and prosperity for the good, and even work miracles. The supernatural force that enables him to carry out his task is of the same kind that moves the stars in their courses and ensures the regular return of the seasons. Thus graceful young women or youths with angel's wings personifying the various times of the year often appear on triumphal arches beside the figure of Victory, or on tombs, where they symbolize the hoped for resurrection.

Symbolism in the home

Symbolism entered so much into the Romans' way of thinking that sometimes it even influenced the way people decorated their houses. In this sphere, however, the methods of exegeses we have just discussed are less easy to apply. Were the frescoes in Pompeian houses intended simply to delight the eye, or did they express religious beliefs? K. Schefold supports the second of these hypotheses in a brilliant book that has caused a great deal of controversy. He observed that the various pictures decorating the Pompeian houses often fall into a sequence linked together by an underlying idea. The gods and heroes whose exploits are shown were not chosen at random; for example, Bacchus, Apollo, Venus, Diana, and Isis were particularly popular. There seems to be a definite link here with the work of the poets of the time: for example, the paintings of the third style could be used as illustrations to Ovid and Horace, while the dramatic frescoes of the fourth style often deal with subjects treated in Seneca's tragedies. These writers—and particularly Horace and Seneca—were not inclined to treat mythology simply as a source of time-honoured material, but derived moral and philosophical lessons from it, using it to some extent as a present-day preacher uses the Bible. The Roman aristocracy's attachment to the Greek literary traditions was not merely a matter of aesthetic appreciation, but had a religious element. As we have seen in the section on sarcophagi, the Romans considered art as a means of ennobling the soul and attaining the divine.

Superstition: protective images

Not everybody, however, was capable of such an elevated view of things. The household decorations, and particularly the mosaics, often bear witness to much more crude beliefs, some of which have endured to this day. One is belief in the evil eye—a belief that is still widespread in all the Mediterranean countries. To keep away the baneful *individus*—the possessor of the evil eye—phylacteries were manufactured in great numbers. These were often obscene, for obscenity was considered as a means of chasing evil spirits. The number of phalli to be seen on thresholds and street corners—which were considered as particularly dangerous spots—often give the uninstructed visitor to an ancient Roman town the impression that the inhabitants indulged in unbridled sexuality, whereas their morals were not very different from our own. Whatever the guides may say, these objects had nothing to do with brothels, but were "remedies" against the evil eye. For this, we have direct evidence from Pliny. A mosaic at Antioch shows that there was already a belief in the benign influence of hunchbacks, and in North Africa fish had—and indeed still have—the reputation of promoting fertility. Special powers were also attributed to the peacock, millet-grass, and the rose.

Archaeology and the texts

In the delicate task of interpreting the meaning of buildings and monuments, Roman archaeologists obviously have certain advantages over those studying other civilizations. They do not have to try to fathom the meaning of their discoveries with only common sense or uncertain ethnological data to guide them. Their problem is rather that of finding the appropriate clue in a mass of written material. A deep knowledge of Latin literature is needed not only when it comes to interpreting the symbolism of a relief or a design, but at every stage of the excavation. The archaeologist in charge must have a solid classical background; others who are less familiar with the Latin authors may also be of great service, but only if they do not mind working in a team. The day is past when excavations were conducted by a single scholar who appropriated the finds to himself. A thorough and detailed investigation can be achieved only by a collective effort, and the rapid publication of the results is a duty incumbent on every archaeologist.

The contribution of Roman Archaeology

Is it really necessary to devote so much attention to the civilization of Rome? Some people think that its literature tells us all we need to know about it, and that archaeology would do better to concentrate on ancient peoples who made no contribution to our own tradition, such as those of the East or of Pre-Colombian America. To convince these sceptics, it should be sufficient to point out the extent to which archaeology has changed our image of "the grandeur that was Rome".

Reassessment of the Imperial Era

At the beginning of this book we noted that 18th-century scholars were primarily interested in the earlier periods of Roman history. For them, Roman civilization reached its peak between the 5th and 3rd centuries

170

C·HERENNIVS·CHARITO·VOTVM·SOLVIT
ΕΡΕΝΝΙΟΣΧΑΡΙΤΩΝ·ΕΥΞΑΜΕΝΟΣ

DIIS · MANIBVS
M·IVNIO·PERSO·PATRONO
ET·M·IVNIO SATIRO
ET·M·IVNIO IVSTO
ET·IVNIAE PIAE
FECIT
IVNIA·VENVSTA·CONIVGI·SVO
ET·FILIIS · DVLCISSIMIS
VNA · CVM PHARNACE·LIB

174,175

←182
185→

←183
184

B.C., in the period when the Republic had triumphed over its neighbours, conquered Italy, and broken the power of Carthage. They considered the 1st century, with its civil wars, as the beginning of a long decline that the brief respite from tyranny and bloodshed under the Antonines was powerless to stop. Then, with the advent of the Severans, the Mediterranean world finally sank into barbarism, to emerge again only with the Renaissance.

This was still more or less the humanist point of view at the end of the 19th century. A now-forgotten writer, E. Gebhardt, who was a member of the French School at Rome, gave the title "In the Twilight of the Ancient World" to a novel set in the reign of Tiberius. Even today, a number of people think of the Imperial Era as a time of misery, oppression, and intellectual and moral decline. On the other hand, the idea of "Republican virtue" has lost much of its appeal, and in these anticolonialist days we are struck more by the brutality of the Roman conquests than by the qualities of the conquerors. While Tacitus has maintained his reputation, the same cannot be said of Livy or Plutarch. In a recent article, J. Guéhenno even reproached P. Grimal for choosing "Roman Civilization" as the title of a book.

This attitude strikes us as unduly pessimistic; when you have spent much of your life studying the material remains of the Empire, you can no longer believe that its inhabitants lived in terror, suffering, and immorality. The wealthy and the noble spent a large part of their fortunes on the building of fora, temples, libraries, baths, and theatres, where all their fellow-citizens, including the paupers and the slaves, could enjoy the benefits of Roman ease and culture. Few civilizations, even when they have been based on religions preaching piety and charity, have produced such disinterested benefactors. The sculptures and epitaphs on the tombs show that the views held by the great majority of the inhabitants of the Empire on such subjects as sexual morality, family life, and the value of hard work could scarcely be improved upon. They permit us to set the much-quoted diatribes of the Roman moralists in their proper perspective and to realize that, in the usual way of such writers, they vented their wrath on a few special cases that were a source of scandal simply because they were exceptional.

Finally, studies of the buildings and monuments of the Empire from the artistic standpoint have shown that some of the most remarkable were produced during periods that have been universally condemned by the historians, such as the 3rd and 4th centuries A.D.

It would be foolish to pretend that archaeology offers us a completely idyllic view of life in the Empire. The recent discovery at El Djem in Tunisia of a mosaic representing men—probably prisoners of war—being eaten alive by leopards in an arena is a salutary reminder of acts of cruelty whose public nature rendered them all the more appalling. But should the civilizations of, say, China or 17th-century France be judged by their atrocities? To sum up, archaeology has shown that the notion of the decadence of the Roman Empire is largely an arbitrary one. This has been borne out by textual criticism, which has demonstrated, for example, that the unfavourable view of the 1st-century Emperors presented by Tacitus is a slanted one and can be explained in terms of his own social origins.

New light on the beginnings of Rome

As regards the beginnings of Rome, the archaeologist has succeeded in correcting the assumptions of certain over-sceptical critics. Fifty years ago, the traditions assembled by such historians as Livy on the subject of the early kings were not taken very seriously. The discovery of the Etruscan temples of the Tarquins and of a paved forum dating from the beginning of the 6th century B.C., together with the re-emergence of the huts and tombs of the companions of Romulus, proved that the scholars of the Augustan period had, in fact, quite an accurate idea of the early development of Rome. In 1965, gold plaques with dedications in Phoenician and Etruscan were brought to light by Pallotino in Caere; they had been made for a Tyrrhenian king, Thefarius Velunias, who governed the city at the beginning of the 5th century. This exceptional discovery provides new and weighty evidence in support of those who believe that Polybius was correct in dating the first treaty between Rome and Carthage from 509 B.C., since it proves that an Etruscan town, a few miles from Rome, contained a large Punic colony.

Excavations have thrown scarcely any light on the troubled times that followed the expulsion of the kings, though the Danish scholar E. Gjerstad has drawn an important historical conclusion from his study of Greek pottery, namely that the Etruscan dynasty must have fallen in the middle of the 5th century B.C.—i.e., some fifty years later than was generally thought—because the pottery suddenly stopped being imported round about that time. This is a somewhat controversial matter, for, not only is the date when the imports of Greek pottery ceased not absolutely certain (R. Bloch places it round about 480–470 B.C.), but this phenomenon was not confined to Rome (it was also observed at Carthage, for example) and it is probably not legitimate to explain it in terms of the internal history of the Republic.

It need not be assumed, however, that archaeology can do nothing to elucidate the history of the beginnings of the Roman conquest. The current exploration of the great sanctuary of Lavinium will probably throw light on the complex relationships between Rome and the league formed by the other Latin towns. The discovery at Veii of statuettes of Aeneas carrying his father Anchises away from the burning city of Ilion proves that the myth retold by Virgil dates back to the 6th century—not the 3rd, as textual criticism has suggested. Studies of the distribution of Campanian pottery, though still at an early stage, have already demonstrated that in the 3rd century B.C. the Italian Confederation had become an industrial and commercial power of the first order. In the light of this finding, the Punic Wars can no longer be considered as a struggle in which a naval power based on trade confronted a military power based on agriculture and rather backward in the economic sphere. The Temple of the Mother of the Gods erected on the Palatine at the end of the war with Hannibal and the group of temples on the Largo Argentina bear tangible witness to the crisis of conscience that shook Rome at the very moment of its triumph over its most formidable opponent. Thus archaeology can bring evidence to bear on all the crucial problems of Roman history, and this evidence is often decisive. The historian can no longer draw on it solely to obtain a few portraits of great men—until recently, often wrongly identified—and views of famous monuments to illustrate a text. Today, in fact, every historian must be an archaeologist, just as every archaeologist must be a historian.

CHRONOLOGY

During the 8th century B.C.	Foundations of huts on the Palatine, Necropolis in the Forum.
753	Traditional date of founding of Rome by Romulus.
c. 650	First paved Forum.
6th century B.C.	The Etruscans (the Tarquin dynasty) masters of Rome. Temples of the Olitorium Forum. Architectonic terra cotta in the Forum and on the the Palatine.
509	Temple dedicated to Jupiter on the Capitoline hill.
c. 500	Bronze she-wolf on the Capitoline hill.
390	Sack of Rome by the Gauls.
Second half of the 4th century B.C.	The artist Fabius Pictor (decoration in the Temple of Salus, 303 B.C.).
c. 300 ?	Bronze bust of Brutus. Temple C built on the Largo Argentina.
4th and 3rd centuries B.C.	Boxes in engraved bronze produced in Praeneste and Rome.
First half of 3rd century	Heavy bronze coins struck in Rome, and silver drachmae made in Campania in the name of Rome.
260	Rostral Column of Duilius.
Second half of 3rd century ?	Temple A on the Largo Argentina.
185	Cato builds the Porcia Basilica.
180–160	Alterations made to the square on the Largo Argentina.
168	Monument at Delphi by Aemilius Paullus.
2nd century B.C.	First pictorial style at Herculaneum and Pompeii.

144 B.C.	The Marcia Aqueduct built.
142	Aemilius' Bridge on the Tiber.
121	Fornix Fabianus in the Forum.
82	Sulla dictator.
c. 80	The Tabularium. The temples on the Largo Argentina restored. Sulla's Triumphal Column on the Capitoline. The Praeneste Sanctuary restored. Pompeii a Roman colony. The Casa del Fauno; the Alexander mosaic.
80-60	First phase of second pictorial style: the House of the Griffins on the Palatine. Edifice at Glanum: capitals of pillars inscribed with figure drawings.
55	Pompey's Theatre and Temple of Venus Victrix.
After 54	Works during Caesar's aedileship: the Basilica Julia, the Temple of Venus Genetrix and the Forum Iulium.
c. 50	Villa of the Mysteries and Labyrinth House, Pompeii. Foundations known as those of the Domitius Ahenobarbus.
46	Caesar's Triumphal Altar, the "Kbor Klib", near Zama (Tunisia).
39	Agrippa dedicates the Temple of Valetudo at Glanum.
After 30	Manufacture of sigillated pottery begins in Arezzo and succeeds the type known as Campanian pottery.
29	The temple of the deified Caesar (Divus Iulius) in the Forum of Rome. Arch of Augustus in the Forum.
27	Temple of Apollo on the Palatine: Gate of Rimini.

25 B.C.	Augustus' trophies at Saint-Bertrand-de-Comminges.
20	Prototype of the bronze statue of Augustus at Primaporta.
30–15	Last phase of the second style: Augustus' House on the Palatine; Farnesina.
c. 15	The Theatre at Arles. Beginning of the third style: Agrippa Postumus' Villa at Boscotrecase.
Before 12	The Maison Carrée at Nîmes.
13–9	The Ara Pacis built.
6	Trophy of Turbia.
2	The Forum of Augustus and the Temple of Mars Ultor completed.
c. Beginning of this era	Arch of Carpentras.
6 A.D.	The Dioscures' Temple in the Forum rebuilt.
16	Tiberius' Arch in the Forum.
27	Arch of Orange.
Between 23 and 27	The "Grand Camée de France".
30	Statue of Tiberius at Pozzuoli.
32	Great Temple of Bel at Palmyra.
43	Claudius dedicates the Pietas Augusta Altar.
Under Claudius	The "romantic" phase in the third style: House of Amandus the priest.
c. 50	Neo-Pythagorean basilica at the Porta Maggiore.
63	Earthquake at Pompeii.
c. 60	Nero's Domitius Transitoria.
64	The burning of Rome.
64–68	Fabullus decorates the Domus Aurea. Early decorations in the House of the Vettii

	in Pompeii by Joseph II and Pinarius Cerealis, *palaestra* and *macellum*.
70–79 A.D.	Reign of Vespasian: last phase of the fourth style at Pompeii (House of Octavius Quartio); Temple of Vespasian. Basilica at Herculaneum. Frescoes at Stabiae.
77	Cadastre at Orange.
On August 24th, 79	Pompeii and Herculaneum destroyed.
80	Dedication of the Coliseum. Titus' Baths.
81	Titus' Arch.
81–96	Domitian's reign: Domus Flavia on the Palatine; reliefs in the Chancellery, trophies said to belong to Marius. Mosaics at Zliten, Tripolitania.
97–98	Nerva dedicates the Forum Transitorium built by Domitian.
100	Timgad founded.
Between 104 and 110	Trajan's Baths.
109	Trophy of Adamklissi.
112	Trajan's Forum dedicated. Baths of Buticosus at Ostia (beginnings of the black-and-white mosaic with large figure design).
c. 110	Mosaic on the Judgement of Paris at Antioch (Louvre Museum).
114–117	Arch of Benevento.
116	Forum and Arch at Mactar.
After 117	Trajan's Baths at Acholla (Tunisia).
117–138	Reign of Hadrian: building of the Tibur Villa from 125 onwards. "Hadrian's town" built at Athens (gateway). In Spain, Italica rebuilt.
c. 124	Hadrian's Pantheon.

135 A.D.	Temple of Venus and Rome.
c. 135	Monument to Hadrian's hunts.
137	Serapeum and adjoining buildings, Ostia.
139	Hadrian's Mausoleum.
145	Temple of Faustina at the Forum.
146–162	Baths of Antoninus at Carthage.
150	Temples at Baalbek.
155	Theatre at Aspendus.
c. 160	Great relief on the Celsus Library at Ephesus, built in honour of that dynasty.
c. 165	Victories won by Carthage. Sarcophagi with scenes on wars against the Galatae. Flowering of African mosaic work: House of the Laberii at Oudna, Neptune's Triumph at Acholla, House of the Dionysian Procession at El Djem; great Bacchic mosaic at Djemila.
175	Triumphal Arch of Marcus Aurelius on the Capitoline (reliefs were later used again in Constantine's Arch).
180	Column of Marcus Aurelius.
c. 190	Sarcophagus of Portonaccio (scenes from wars against the Teutons) and Sarcophagus of the Dionysian Triumph (now in Walters Art Gallery, Baltimore).
c. 200	Christian house in Dura Europos.
204	Gate of the Silversmiths at the Forum Boarium.
205	Arch of Septimius Severius at the Roman Forum and at Leptis Magna.
Before 21	The Septizonium on the Palatine which was copied in several towns, especially in Africa.

c. 211 A.D.	Mosaics in the House of Virgil at Hadrumetum (Sousse, Tunisia).
211–217	Reign of Caracalla: Severian Forum completed and the great Basilica in Leptis built.
Between 200 and 230	Early paintings in the catacombs. Sarcophagi portraying lion hunting.
c. 235	Sarcophagus with Dionysius and the Seasons (now in New York); sarcophagi from Saint-Médard-d'Eyrans (in the Louvre). The earliest Christian sarcophagi date from this time.
c. 235	The Coliseum at El Djem (Tunisia).
235	Fall of Alexander Severus; beginnings of the "realistic" portraits.
c. 240	Magerius mosaic at Smirat (Tunisia).
After 245	Paintings in the Synagogue in Dura Europos.
248	Rome's millennium. Philippopolis built in Syria (mosaic at Aion).
251	Sarcophagus of Hostilian (last battle sarcophagus).
256	Destruction of Dura Europos.
260–268	Reign of Gallienus. Sarcophagi with portraits of philosophers. In Thugga (Dugga, Tunisia): Lycian Baths, House of Dionysius and Ulysses, underground houses of Bulla Regia.
275	Palmyra destroyed.
From 271 onwards	Building of the Aurelian enclosure and the Temple of the Sun in Rome.
276–277	Great Teutonic invasion of Gaul, most of the cities destroyed; a great number of monuments were completely wiped out and their debris went into building enclosures around towns which had grown steadily smaller over the last quarter of the century; the main rural sanctuaries were similarly annihilated.

284–305 A.D.	Reign of Diocletian who organized the Tetrarchy.
293	Monument of the Decennalia at the Roman Forum.
299	Palace of Galerius at Salonika with Triumphal Arch and Mausoleum, transformed into the Church of St. George.
305	Palace of Diocletian at Split.
After 306	Imperial Basilica at Trier; painted roof in the Imperial Palace of the same town.
311	Carthage and numerous African towns destroyed.
312	Arch of Constantine at the Roman Forum.
312–319	Church of Bishop Theodore at Aquileia.
315–320	Helen, Constantine's mother, founds the Church of the Nativity at Bethlehem; the Sanctuary of the Holy Sepulchre built in Jerusalem. Carthage rebuilt; the "House of the Horses", headquarters for new recruits in the army. Numerous mosaics depicting hunting scenes in Africa. Villa of the Piazza Armerina in Sicily.
319	Lateran Basilica and Baptistry.
After 326	St. Peter's in the Vatican.
327–330	Building of Constantinople.
350	Mausoleum of Constantius at Centcelles, near Tarragona.
c. 355	Mausoleum of Constantia, Via Nomentana (Church of St. Constantia).
356	Paintings in the Domitilla Catacombs, depicting St. Petronella.

BIBLIOGRAPHY

General

R. CAGNAT, V. CHAPOT, *Manuel d'archéologie romaine*, 2 vols. Paris, 1920. (A rather summary work, now dated).

A. GRENIER, *Manuel d'archéologie gallo-romaine*. An exhaustive work on Gaul containing much information on Roman archaeology in general; unfortunately it has not been completed. Part I: Generalities and military works. 1931. Part II: Archaeology at ground-level (roads and land development). 1934. Part III: Architecture (town planning and monuments; ludi et circenses). 1958.

Architecture

L. CREMA, *Architettura Romana*. 1959.

Arts

There is a steadily growing body of material available on the history of Roman art. Cf. the author's *Art romain*, 1962, and the bibliographical summary published each year in the *Revue des études latines*, archaeological Bulletin.

Excavations

Excavations and publications are recorded in *Fasti Archaeologici*, an annual publication of the International Association for Classical Studies. Also consult the *Archäologischer Anzeiger*, an annual supplement to the *Jahrbuch des Deutschen Archäologischen Instituts*.

Main Sites

ITALY

The *Itinerari dei Musei e Monumenti d'Italia* published by the Italian Ministry of Education (Ministero della Pubblica Istruzione) should be consulted first. The collection comprises over 100 fascicules written by leading specialists. Special mention must be made of the following: P. ROMANELLI, *Il Foro Romano*; S. AURIGEMMA, *Le Terme de Diocleziano ed il Museo Nazionale Romano*; A. MAIURI, *Pompéi et Herculanum*; G. CALZA, *Ostia*; G. IACOPI, *Il Santuario della Fortuna Primigenia e il Museo Prenestino*; G.V. GENTILI, *La Villa Imperiale di Piazza Armerina*.

Rome

G. LUGLI, *I Monumenti Antichi di Roma e suburbio*, 3 vols., 1930–1938. Vol. I was re-written and completely revised and published under the title *Il Centro monumentale* in 1946.

Ostia

R. MEIGGS, *Roman Ostia*. 1960.

Verona

P. MARCONI, *Verona Romana*. 1937.

Padua

C. GASPAROTTO, *Padova Romana*. 1951.

Aquileia

A regular account of discoveries is given in the review entitled *Aquileia nostra*.

G. BRUSIN, P. L. ZOVATTO, *Monumenti Paleocristiani di Aquileia*.

GAUL

The fundamental work in this field is *Le recueil général des statues et bas-reliefs de la Gaule* (i.e. Comprehensive inventory of statues and bas-reliefs in Gaul), by E. ESPÉRANDIEU and continued by R. LANTIER. H. STERN has compiled a *Recueil des Mosaïques de la Gaule*. The review

Gallia publishes the annual reports of the Directors of archaeological circonscriptions and the most important studies on archaeology in France. A record of developments in Gallo-Roman architecture is published annually in the *Revue des études anciennes* by P.M. DUVAL.

H.P. EYDOUX describes the large-scale excavations in a lively manner in his various works: *La France Antique, Monuments et trésors de la Gaule, Hommes et Dieux de la Gaule, Lumières sur la Gaule*, and *Résurrection de la Gaule*.

Glanum (Saint-Rémy-de-Provence)
H. ROLLAND, *Fouilles de Glanum*. Vol. I, 1946; vol. II, 1958.

Arles
L. CONSTANS, *Arles Antique*. 1913.

Nîmes
J.C. BALTY, *Etudes sur la Maison Carrée de Nîmes*. 1967.
R. NAUMANN, *Der Quellbezirk von Nîmes*. 1937.

Lyons
A. AUDIN, *Lyon, miroir de Rome dans les Gaules*. 1965.

Périgueux
L. LERAT, *Vesontio*. Vol. I.

Bordeaux
R. ÉTIENNE, *Bordeaux antique*. 1962.

Paris
P.M. DUVAL, *Paris Antique*. 1961.

Strasbourg
J.J. HATT, *Strasbourg au temps des Romains*. 1953.

ROMAN GERMANIA

Inventory of the excavations in *Germania*, a review published by the Rö-misch-Germanische Kommission which also edited an illustrated atlas: *Germania Romana* (1924–1930).

R. LAUR BELART, *Führer durch Augusta Raurica*. 1948.

E. VIRIEUX, *Avenches, cité romaine*. 1959.

BRITAIN

The *Journal of Roman Studies* publishes a regular report on excavations.

I.A. RICHMOND, *A Handbook of the Roman Wall in Britain*. 1947.

SPAIN

A comprehensive bibliography of Roman archaeology in Spain in R. ÉTIENNE, *Le culte impérial dans la péninsule ibérique*, (pp. 543–544). 1958. Regular reports on excavations appear in the *Archivo Español de Arqueología*.

B. TARACENA, *Arte Romano* (vol. II in the *Ars Hispaniae* series, 1947).

A. GARCIA Y BELLIDO, *Italica*. 1960.

M. ALMAGRO, *Ampurias*. 1947.

Following the Fourth International Archaeological Congress held in Barcelona in 1929 monographs were published on the most important Roman sites in Spain. Included in the collection were J.R. MELIDA, *Merida* and M. GONZALEZ SIMANCAS, *Sagunto*.

PORTUGAL

J.M. BAIRRAIO OLEIRO, *Roteiro de Conimbriga*. 1963.

MOROCCO

M. TARRADELL, *Lixus*. 1959.

R. THOUVENOT, *Volubilis*. 1949.

R. ÉTIENNE, *Le quartier nord-est de Volubilis*. 1960.

ALGERIA

The fundamental works are the *Atlas Archéologique de l'Algérie* and *Les Monuments Antiques de l'Algérie* by S. GSELL.

Inventories of excavations were formerly published in the *Bulletin du Comité des Travaux Historiques et Scientifiques* and by the review *Libyca*. Since 1967, they have been published in the *Antiquités Africaines*.

E. BOESWILLWALD, A. BALLU, R. CAGNAT, *Timgad.* 1905.

C. COURTOIS, *Timgad, antique Tamugadi.* 1951.

J. BARADEZ, *Tipasa.* 1952

E. MAREC, *Hippone la royale.* 1954.

Y. ALLAIS, *Djemila.* 1938.

L. LESCHI, *Djemila, antique Cuicul.* 1949.

S. GSELL, *Khamissa, Mdaourouch, Announa.* 1911.

J. BARADEZ, *Fossatum Africae.* 1949.

TUNISIA

G. PICARD, *La civilisation de l'Afrique Romaine.* 1959.

Catalogue of the principal sites by L. POINSSOT in *Atlas Historique... de Tunisie*, Horizons de France. 1936.

A. AUDOLLENT, *Carthage romaine.* 1901.

G. PICARD, *Carthage.* 1951.

L. POINSSOT, *Ruines de Dougga.* 1958.

G. PICARD, *Civitas Mactaritana.* 1957.

TRIPOLITANIA

R. BIANCHI BANDINELLI, G. CAPUTO, C. VERGARA CAFFA-RELLI, *Leptis Magna*, 1963.

M. SQUARCIAPINO, *Leptis Magna.* 1966.

SYRIA, LEBANON, PALESTINE, JORDAN

There is no satisfactory general work available on Roman civilization in the Orient, nor are there any easily obtainable monographs on the principal sites. The basic work on religious architecture is *Römische Tempel in Syrien* 1938, by D. KRENCKER and W. ZSCHIETZSCHMANN. On Dura, in addition to the various volumes published on the excavations, there is *Dura Europos and its Art*, 1938, by M. ROSTOVTZEFF.

ASIA MINOR and GREECE

On sites in Anatolia cf. Nagel's Guide: *Turkey*.

CORNELIUS C. VERMEULE, *Roman Imperial Art in Greece and Asia Minor*. 1967.

RUMANIA

D. TUDOR, *Oraşe, tirguri şi şate in Dacia Romana*. 1967.

C. and H. DAICOVICIU, *Sarmizegethuza*. 1966.

F. BOBU FLORESCU, *Monumentul de la Adamklissi*, 2nd edition 1960.

YUGOSLAVIA

Split

Tomislav MARASOVIC, *Diocletian's Palace*. 1967.

Pula

Stefan MLAKAR, *Ancient Pula*. 2nd edition 1963.

HUNGARY

E.B. THOMAS, *Römische Villen in Pannonien*. 1964.

LIST OF ILLUSTRATIONS

was several times rebuilt. The restored state in which it was found dates from the time of Septimius Severus (193–211 A.D.).

17 Rome. The Forum. House of the Vestals. View of a section of the courtyard in the "convent" surrounded by pedestals of statues of the most famous vestals.

18 Rome. The Forum. Temple of Castor and Pollux, founded 499 B.C. Rebuilt by Tiberius in 6 A.D.

19 Rome. Caracalla's Baths, the largest establishment of its kind in Rome. Built 212 to 217 A.D.

20 Idem. An example of massive brick architecture. The greatest amount of space was given over to the frigidarium and there was also a large swimming pool.

21 Idem. Note the many niches, similar in effect to baroque architecture.

22 Idem. Pavement mosaics: simple pattern in black-and-white shells. The Baths also have black-and-white and polychrome figure designs in mosaic.

23 Idem. Large circular room containing the baths; vaulted roof with cupola.

24 Rome. Trajan's Market. 113 A.D. Extensive and very well preserved markets are attached to Trajan's Forum and take up one end of the Quirinal. This curved façade inspired baroque architects.

25 Rome. The Palatine. The so-called racecourse in the Flavian Palace was actually an enclosed garden.

26 Rome. The Palatine. Flavian's Palace and the fountains on the side of the great peristyle.

27 Rome. Augustus' Forum. The square, inaugurated in 2 B.C., contains the Temple of Mars Ultor and used to hold statues of all the great men in Roman history.

28 Rome. The great Circus in the foreground; Domitian's Palace in the background. Chariot races were held in the hollow of the Circus as early as the 6th century B.C. During the Imperial Era it became a princely duty to preside over the races and the Palace was directly linked to the Circus.

29 Rome. The Coliseum. Completed in 80 B.C. Its name is due, not to its size, but to "Nero's Colossus" which was located nearby. The site was earlier a pool in the gardens of the Domus Aurea.

30   Rome. *The Coliseum in the background and in the foreground the Temple of Venus and Rome. Built by Hadrian (117–138), this huge double temple resembles a Greek temple in external appearance, but the vaulted brick interior followed the principles of Roman architecture.*

31   Rome. *Mausoleum of Augustus. 14 A.D. Augustus' tomb is a huge tumulus, doubtlessly inspired by Etruscan mausoleums. The ashes of all the Emperors up to Nero's time were deposed there.*

32   *Ostia.* Decumanus maximus *near the theatre. The main street in Ostia, running parallel to the old bed of the river Tiber. It runs straight for 900 metres, then turns south to meet the Porta Marina.*

33   *Ostia. Eastern portico of the Corporations' square paved with mosaics. This square, beside the theatre, contained the shipping companies' offices. The mosaics with their emblems date from the last years of the 2nd century A.D.*

34   *Ostia. The Forum, centre of the political life of the colony founded in 335 B.C., was completely reconstructed under Hadrian (117–138).*

35   *Ostia. General aerial view. The Capitol and Forum are in the centre surrounded by blocks of brick buildings built during the 2nd century A.D.*

36   *Ostia. Temple of Hercules. Built in the reign of Sulla (80 B.C.) and restored under Hadrian; it was one of the most important sanctuaries.*

37   *Ostia. The Theatre. Built under Augustus, it was restored at the beginning of the 3rd century A.D.*

38   *Ostia. Aerial view of the Roman theatre. In the foreground, the theatre whose* cavea *is supported by a vaulting system; the Corporations' square is to the rear, lined by the offices of 70 shipping companies.*

39   *Ostia. The theatre. A mask symbolizing Tragedy, probably from the beginning of the 3rd century A.D.*

40   *Ostia. Trajan's* schola, *the seat of one of the many corporations which were active in the town. Its present state dates from the beginning of the 3rd century A.D.*

41   *Ostia. Baths in the Forum: the Palaestra. Ostia had many public baths built in the 2nd century. They were used for bathing and also for sports which took place in the palaestrae.*

42   *Ostia. Baths. The brick architecture and décor in black-and-white figure pattern, are characteristic of the 2nd century A.D.*

43   *Ostia. Street of the Balconies. 2nd century A.D. The inhabitants of Ostia, like the Romans, mostly lived in rented houses which were divided into apartments.*

44   *Ostia. Street of the Fountain. Large straight streets lined by brick houses with identical façades. Ostia in the Antonine period had already the aspect of a modern city of today.*

45   *Ostia. Façade of the Horrea Epagathiana. The offices of a large business society which was run by freed slaves. 2nd century A.D.*

46   *Ostia. Jars in the Horrea. The huge* dolia *stored the goods received for consumption in Rome. 2nd century A.D.*

47   *Ostia. House of the Columns. Courtyard in a 4th century A.D. house.*

48   *Ostia. Grotto of Love. The grave crisis in the 3rd century put an end to Ostia's economic activity. At the end of the Empire, the town was a holiday resort for important Roman families who built luxurious residences adorned with fountains, similar to that illustrated here.*

49   *Ostia. House of the Fish. Another example of an aristocratic residence of the 4th century A.D.*

50   *Timgad. Trajan's arch and the* decumanus maximus. *Trajan's arch, gateway to the colony founded in 101, is dedicated to its founding Emperor but actually dates from the following century. It opens onto the* decumanus, *the main street in the town.*

51   *Timgad. General view of the town founded by Trajan. Remarkable for its geometrically regular ground plan. Suburbs which were not so strictly planned later developed around the city.*

52   *Timgad. The Forum, centre of the town's political life. This was a "lay" Forum and had no sanctuary of any importance.*

53   *Timgad. View of the Capitol's temple. The Capitol was surprisingly omitted from the colony's original ground plan.*

54   *Timgad. North* cardo. *While the* decumanus *cut across Timgad from East to West, the cardo leads up to, but not beyond, the Forum. This was the only deviation from the strictly planned Roman town made by Trajan's town-planner.*

55 *Timgad. The temple of the Capitol. This was built later in the western suburbs and to compensate for the delay it was planned on a very large scale. The monument was restored in 365 A.D.*

56 *Carthage. Antoninus' Baths. The Carthage Baths are the only ones to have a ground-floor entirely given over to rooms for the works. This is the only part of the building which has survived.*

57 *Idem. A colossal capital. Middle of the 2nd century A.D.*

58 *Sbeitla. The Capitol. One of the three temples which form the Capitol of Sagetula (today known as Sbeitla). Second half of the 2nd century A.D.*

59 *Sbeitla. Arch of the Tetrarchy, dedicated to Diocletian and his colleagues between 293 and 305 A.D.*

60 *Baalbek. Interior of a small temple known as Bacchus' Temple. A type of baroque décor, not exclusively Syrian, but evident in numerous temples in Rome and the West.*

61 *Baalbek. General view. Construction of the vast ensemble of temples in Baalbek was spaced out over a period stretching from the beginning of the 1st century A.D. to the beginning of the 3rd century.*

62 *Byblos. Roman theatre. 2nd century A.D. Theatres built during the Imperial Era in the eastern part of the Empire reveal a design which is midway between that of the Roman and Greek theatres.*

63 *Thugga (Dugga). The Capitol, c. 170 A.D. Note the height of the lateral walls, a technique in common use in Africa.*

64 *Thugga (Dugga). The Roman theatre built under Marcus Aurelius (161–180 A.D.).*

65 *Sabratha. The theatre. The stage décor has been restored. Severian period (193–211 A.D.). Typical example of baroque architecture.*

66 *Volubilis. Arch of Caracalla (211–217 A.D.).*

67 *Volubilis. The Basilica dating from the beginning of the 3rd century A.D.*

68 *Leptis Magna. Caracalla's Basilica, completed in 216 A.D. Pillar in the foreground richly carved and ornamented with a vine leaf design and scenes from the Dionysian legend.*

69 *Saint-Rémy-de-Provence (Glanum). Sanctuary of the Goddess of Goodness. Second half of the 1st century B.C.*

70 *Saalburg. Near Bad Homburg vor der Höhe are the reconstituted head-quarters of a Roman camp in Germania. Period of Caracalla (211–217 A.D.).*

71 *Trier. Porta Nigra. Façade decorated with arcaded windows. Beginning of the 3rd century A.D.*

72 *Histria. Baths. the palaestra. 3rd–4th century. The towns on the Black Sea founded by the Greeks adopted the Roman way of life during the Imperial Era. The Baths, in particular, were built along Western lines.*

73 *Dinogetia. Baths. 4th century. A small swimming pool at the end of the Empire replaced the huge 2nd century installations which could no longer be supplied with water.*

74 *Roman Sarmizegetuza (Ulpia Traiana). Roman paving, 2nd–3rd century. Trajan moved the capital of his vanquished enemy, Decebalus, down onto the plain and granted it the statute of a Roman colony bearing his own name.*

75 *Adamklissi. Near the great Trophy which commemorates the conquest of Dacia by Trajan a town grew up where Christianity was to develop at an early date: one of the town's churches is illustrated.*

76 *Constanţa. Greek sarcophagus from the Imperial Era from a workshop in Asia Minor. 3rd century A.D.*

77 *Adamklissi. Trophy commemorating the conquest of Dacia by Trajan (101–106 A.D.). The ornamentation was carried out by local artists and is an example of folk art in the service of Imperial propaganda.*

78 *Italica. An aerial view. The homeland of Trajan and Hadrian. Italica, founded earlier by Scipio, was entirely rebuilt due to Imperial generosity after 117.*

79 *Italica. The amphitheatre. One of the largest in the Roman Empire with room for 25,000 spectators.*

80 *Italica. Mosaics. The houses in Italica have yielded up a rich hoard of polychrome mosaics which may be dated from the second half of the 2nd century and from the first half of the 3rd century A.D.*

81 *Ampurias. Mosaic pavements. Emporion, a Greek colony for long confined within its ramparts, expanded after a visit by Caesar. Palaces were then built in the suburbs, paved with black-and-white mosaics in the Italian style.*

82 *Fragment of mural painting. The only vestige of historic Roman painting in the Republican period. This 3rd century fresco doubtlessly represents an episode in the Samnite wars. Museo dei Conservatori, Rome.*

83–86 *The great frieze in the Villa of the Mysteries in Pompeii. 2nd style, c. 60 B.C.*

87 *A nymph surprised by Pan. Pompeii. An erotic Hellenistic theme frequently treated in Roman art. This is an example of Pompeian painting in the 4th style, 63–79 A.D. Naples Museum.*

88 *Hercules tormented by love. Pompeii. The theme is originally Hellenistic but the "romantic" landscape is characteristic of works in the late 3rd style, c. 50 A.D.*

89 *Satyr and nymph. Pompeii. Painting in the 4th style (65–79 A.D.). Note "impressionistic" treatment. Naples Museum.*

90 *Mosaic in Neptune's Baths. Ostia. In the first half of the 2nd century a school of mosaic workers in Ostia decorated the Baths with large scale compositions in black-and-white representing gods and sea-monsters.*

91 *Mosaic of the western portico of the Corporations' square. Ostia.*

92 *Mosaic of Neptune's Baths. Ostia, c. 140 A.D.*

93 *Idem. The decoration of Neptune's Baths is the masterpiece of the Ostian School.*

94 *Mosaics in Caracalla's Baths, Rome. (211–217 A.D.). These are the last examples of the great creations of the Romano-Ostian school of the 2nd century. The black-and-white pattern then disappears and is replaced by polychrome mosaic.*

95 *Idem.*

96 *Idem. The winged spirit riding a dolphin, although in the 2nd century tradition and in black-and-white, already shows the anatomical style of figures dating from late Antiquity.*

97 *Mosaics on the eastern portico of the Corporations' square at Ostia (180–190 A.D.).*

98 *Idem. At the end of the second century, scenes from daily life appear with increasing frequency in mosaics.*

99 *Mosaic in Fortunatus' inn. Ostia. Like other similar mosaics from the same period (3rd century) this was intended to bring good luck to the inn-keeper and his clients.*

100 *Mosaic in the Villa of the Fish. Ostia. Detail of an Ostian mosaic of the 4th century A.D.*

101 *Polychrome mosaic. Ostia. Another example of a mosaic from the 4th century A.D.*

102 *Detail of a mosaic. Acholla (now Botria), c. 160–170 A.D.*

103 *Pylochrome mosaic with geometric design. Ostia. This elegant floral design is a late imitation (mid-3rd century?) of a 2nd century theme.*

104 *Black-and-white mosaic representing a shield of scales and the head of Medusa. Ostia. Mid-2nd century A.D.*

105 *Venus and Mercury. Gighti. 3rd century A.D. In the 3rd century, chessboard-design mosaics were fashionable, each square representing a different scene. Bardo Museum, Tunis.*

106 *Diana the Huntress. Utica. Early 3rd century A.D. Mythological scene treated in the "impressionistic" style fashionable c. 200 A.D. Bardo Museum, Tunis.*

107 *A basket of flowers. La Chebba, c. 200 A.D. Detail of a mosaic with inter-locking design combining curvilinear shapes and rounded or oval medallions. Bardo Museum, Tunis.*

108 *Hound chasing a hare. Carthage. 3rd century A.D. In the 3rd century hunting scenes are extremely frequent in African mosaics. Bardo Museum, Tunis.*

109 *Peacock. Thuburbo Maius. 3rd century A.D. The heavy acanthus foliage is characteristic of the taste of the time. The peacock, a propitious animal, is very frequently represented. Bardo Museum, Tunis.*

110 *Satyr and Bacchante. El Djem, 3rd century A.D. The cult of Dionysius was very popular in Africa and is a recurring theme in mosaics. Bardo Museum, Tunis.*

111 *Venus at her toilet. Thuburbo Maius. 3rd century A.D. The theme of Venus' beautification is a frequent one in the African repertory of the early 3rd century, at the end of Antiquity. Bardo Museum, Tunis.*

112   *Polychrome mosaic: masks. Copy of a Hellenistic model executed in the
2nd century A.D. This mosaic represents two comic masks, one depicting
a young woman, the other an old man. Capitoline Museum, Rome.*

113   *Polychrome mosaic: doves. Found in Hadrian's villa at Tibur, the mosaic
is a copy of a masterpiece by Sosus of Pergamum. 2nd century A.D. Along-
side works expressing the spirit of their day are found, in every period,
and in all branches of the arts including mosaics, pastiches which are sometimes very faithful copies of antique models. Capitoline Museum, Rome.*

114   *Mosaic: farm. Tabarka. End of 4th century A.D. Mosaics in the 3rd
and 4th centuries often represent important aristocratic domains. Bardo
Museum, Tunis.*

115   *Coronation of Venus. Elles. Mid-2nd century A.D. This mosaic is not readily
decipherable: the inscription remains a mystery; it refers in any case to
the horses in a team competing in a circus. Two of these race-
horses are represented as female centaurs who are crowning Venus, pro-
tectress of the stable to which the chariot belonged. Bardo Museum, Tunis.*

116   *Dionysian mosaic. Satyr and Maenad. Cologne. Detail of a Bacchic mosaic.
Note the interlocking pattern, framing the medallion with figure design,
typical of mosaics after the end of the 3rd century A.D.*

117   *Idem. Detail. Compare with the treatment of a similar theme in Pompeian
painting (no. 86).*

118   *Dionysian mosaic: panther. Cologne, c. 230 A.D.*

119   *Mosaic in the villa of the Piazza Armerina: a big game hunt (detail).
Tigress caught by a mirror. Early 4th century A.D.*

120   *Idem. Big game hunt (detail). A solider of rank reprimands and strikes
a hunter.*

121   *Idem. Hunt for small game (detail). Bird catchers trapping birds with
snares.*

122   *Idem. Big game hunt (detail). A high-ranking dignitary in uniform.*

123   *Idem. Hunt (detail). Deer caught in nets.*

124   *Idem. Hunt (detail). Return of the hunters.*

125   Idem. *Endymion's sleep.*

126   Four seasons' mosaic. Carthage, c. 320 A.D. Detail of a mosaic representing
a black "witch doctor" celebrating a fertility rite.

127   Detail from a mosaic in the "House of the Horses". Carthage, antiquarium,
c. 320 A.D. The frieze portraying this wader shows children hunting small
animals in the amphitheatre.

128   Silverware treasure at Hildesheim. A silver bowl portraying Athena.
Found in Germany, south of Hanover, the hoard comprised 70 silver vases
from the Christian era. They had either been stolen by a robber chief or
offered by the Roman merchants who often visited the country.

129   Idem.

130   Idem.

131   African vase. Tunisia. First half of the 3rd century A.D. Louvre Museum,
Paris.

132   Silverware hoard at Kaiseraugst. A fish dish in silver. 4th century A.D.

133   Idem. Silver dish. Inlaid and partly gilded border and central medallion.
The central medallion shows a cliff by the sea. The edge is decorated with
four hunting scenes alternating with four strips of geometric design. Compare with contemporary mosaics in the villa of the Piazza Armerina (Pl.
119 to 125).

134   Idem. Detail. Palace by the sea, similar to that of Diocletian at Split.

135   Vase from Arezzo. This type of pottery made in Tuscany spread throughout
the entire Roman Empire as far afield as India, from 30 B.C. to 50 A.D.
Its potsherds are therefore a sure chronological indication. Louvre Museum,
Paris.

136   "Spinario". Copy of Myron's masterpiece of the 5th century B.C. made
in the middle of the 1st century B.C. Capitoline Museum, Rome.

137   Underwater exploration at Mahdia. Head, c. 80 B.C. This piece, carved
in Greece, had been forwarded with a shipment of objets d'art from Athens
to Italy. The ship foundered off the Tunisian coast and was explored between 1907 and 1913, then again between 1951 and 1955. Bardo Museum,
Tunis.

138 *Idem. Head of Pan.*

139 *Bronze copy of a 5th century Greek statue which decorated Piso's villa, the Villa of the Papyri, in Herculaneum, excavated in the 18th century.*

140 *Idem.*

141 *Portrait of a man. Middle of the 3rd century B.C. Museo dei Conservatori, Rome.*

142 *Ganymede. Marble. End of 2nd century A.D. Statue found in Carthage theatre. Bardo Museum, Tunis.*

143 *Head of a boy. Beginning of 1st century A.D. Musée d'art et d'histoire, Geneva.*

144 *Mask of a youth from a bronze statue, Roman period, 1st century A.D. Musée d'art et d'histoire, Geneva.*

145 *Augustus (63 B.C.–14 A.D.). The Emperor is shown here in his old age, in the Christian era. Capitoline Museum, Rome.*

146 *Nero (54–68). Capitoline Museum, Rome.*

147 *Trajan. (98–117). Capitoline Museum, Rome.*

148 *Vespasian (69–79). Capitoline Museum, Rome.*

149 *Hadrian (117–138). Capitoline Museum, Rome.*

150 *Marcus Aurelius (161–180). Capitoline Museum, Rome.*

151 *Septimius Severus (193–211). Capitoline Museum, Rome.*

152 *Plotina (129 A.D.). Capitoline Museum, Rome.*

153 *Salonina, wife of Gallienus, Emperor from 253 to 268. Capitoline Museum, Rome.*

154 *Gallienus (253–268). From Greece. Musée d'art et d'histoire, Geneva.*

155 *Statuette. Museo dei Conservatori, Rome.*

156 *Fortuna and Pontus, c. 190–200 A.D. This type of statue was derived from the statue of "Fortune" at Antioch, by Eutychides (c. 300 B.C.), and was reproduced in all parts of the Empire where it represented maritime towns. Archaeological Museum, Constanţa.*

157 *Centaur, made for Hadrian by a sculptor of the Aphrodisias school in Caria, c. 130 A.D. Capitoline Museum, Rome.*

158 *Statue of the 2nd century A. D. which repeats a 5th century Attic theme. This statue was earlier incorrectly identified as that of the wife of Germanicus, Agrippina the Elder. Capitoline Museum, Rome.*

159 *Silenus bearing a gourd. Bronze. Avenches. These small bronzes were scattered throughout the Empire and originated in a few centres where they were produced on a large scale, one of which was in Alexandria. Musée romain, Avenches.*

160 *Silenus in bronze. Ornament for a chariot. Avenches. Musée romain, Avenches.*

161 *Head of a barbarian in gilded bronze. Avenches. 3rd century A.D. Musée romain, Avenches.*

162 *Celtic divinity. Bronze. Avenches. A remarkable example of folk art where the human face is reproduced without any attempt at realism. Musée romain, Avenches.*

163 *Votive hand consecrated to the god Sabazios, a Thracian god whose cult was known throughout the Empire. These hands were good-luck charms. Avenches. Musée romain, Avenches.*

164 *Knife with folding blade and carved ivory handle depicting gladiators. Avenches. 1st century A.D. The figure on the left is a "Thracian", recognizable by his closed vizor. The gladiator on the right, who appears to be African, is a retiary. Musée romain, Avenches.*

165 *Roman crater discovered at Tinoşu-Prahova, in the Ploeşti region. 2nd–3rd century A.D. Archaeological Museum, Constanţa.*

166 *Sculpture representing a fabulous snake. End of the 2nd century A.D. Archaeological Museum, Constanţa.*

167 *Hind. Plaster. Museo dei Conservatori, Rome.*

168 *Horse. Bronze. Museo dei Conservatori, Rome.*

169 *Sphinx. Stone. Museo dei Conservatori, Rome.*

170 *Funerary stele. Olteniţa. Note the lions and spirits with upturned torches, a symbol of death. The wine leaf design meant that the deceased had been initiated into the mysteries of Bacchus. The name Aurelius and the style of portrait show that this person lived c. 200 A.D. Archaeological Museum, Constanţa.*

171 *Aedicule in white marble with double effigy of Nemesis. Latin and Greek bilingual inscription. End of the 2nd century A.D. Ex-voto from a certain Hereppius Charito to the goddess Nemesis who presided over contests in the amphitheatre. Classicizing art of the Hellenistic provinces. Archaeological Museum, Constanţa.*

172 *Monument dedicated by the widow of a freed slave to her husband, son and daughter, as well as to the master who had freed them. The master's portrait is on top and is characteristic of the Flavian period (70–96 A.D.); portraits of the father and children, in the Trajanian style (98–117 A.D.), are on the body of the cippus. Musei dei Conservatori, Rome.*

173 *Sarcophagus of the second quarter of the 3rd century A.D. Recumbent statues of the deceased on the lid. The woman's hair is done in the fashion prevalent under Alexander Severus (222–232). The bas-relief on the body of the sarcophagus portrays Achilles with the daughters of Lycomedes. Capitoline Museum, Rome.*

174 *Sarcophagus. Myth of Apollo and Marsyas. 140–150 A.D. Museo dei Conservatori, Rome.*

175 *Idem. Detail: the left-hand side of the sarcophagus. Marsyas plays the flute before Apollo.*

176 *Sarcophagus inspired by a combat between Galatian and Greek in Pergamum, c. 160 A.D. Capitoline Museum, Rome.*

177 *Sarcophagus of Saint-Médard-d'Eyrans, c. 230 A.D. The main bas-relief depicts Dionysius finding Ariane at Naxos. This erotic theme was then given a mystical interpretation. Louvre Museum, Paris.*

178 *Central part of a sarcophagus of the first half of the 3rd century A.D., showing Hercules in the garden of the Hesperides. This theme represented the virtuous man's entry into Paradise. Museo dei Conservatori, Rome.*

179 Bas-relief showing the god Mithra. 3rd century A.D. Type of folk sculpture of religious inspiration. In the centre Mithra is seen cutting the throat of the bull whose blood will give birth to the world. Archaeological Museum, Alba Iulia.

180 Ara Pacis Augustae: part of the reconstituted altar dedicated to the Pax Augusta in 9 B.C. Above, Aeneas sacrifices the sow with thirty young; below, ornamentation of acanthus wreaths. The upper relief is inspired by Alexandrine art and the leaf ornamentation by the School of Pergamum.

181 Detail of the Trophy of Adamklissi. 106 A.D. Combats between Dacians and Romans. The Trophy of Adamklissi is one of the very rare official Roman monuments decorated according to the principles of folk art.

182 Bas-reliefs depicting the provinces in the Empire. They come from the temple dedicated to Hadrian who was deified in 138. Museo dei Conservatori, Rome.

183 Idem. Detail: trophy formed by Dacian spoils.

184 Rome: Arch of Titus. A monument which is both triumphal and funerary: the reliefs evoke the Emperor's triumph over the Jews and his apotheosis.

185 Bas-relief: Bacchantes. Thuburbo Maius. Example of classicizing neo-Attic art. Many replicas of this group exist throughout the Empire. End of the 1st century A.D. Bardo Museum, Tunis.

186 Base of a column which bore the statue of the Tetrarchy (285–305). Forum, Rome. The statue represented the sacrifice celebrated in 295 in honour of the 10th anniversary of Diocletian's accession to power.

187 Rome: Constantine's Arch. General view. Dedicated by the Senate and the Roman people in 313 in honour of Constantine's victory over Maxentius. It is the last of the great triumphal monuments in Rome, and the only one to evoke a civil war.

188 Idem. Detail of the reliefs: medaillons representing Hadrian making sacrifice to Diana.

189 Idem. Ornamentation on Constantine's Arch included both reliefs which had been made earlier and previously used, and contemporary sculpture.

190 Idem. Frieze taken from Trajan's Forum giving a symbolic representation of Trajan's victory over the Dacians.

INDEX

Printed in Switzerland

THE TEXT AND ILLUSTRATIONS
IN THIS VOLUME WERE PRINTED
ON THE PRESSES OF NAGEL
PUBLISHERS IN GENEVA

FINISHED IN MAY 1969
BINDING BY NAGEL PUBLISHERS,
GENEVA

OFFSET COLOUR SEPARATION EXECUTED BY
SCHWITTER AG, ZURICH

LEGAL DEPOSIT No 384

PRINTED IN SWITZERLAND

DATE DUE	
NOV 1 4 1997	
MAY 0 2 2001	
OCT 2 2 2002	
DEC 1 3 2002	
DEC 1 3 2004	
NOV 2 0 2009	
DEC 11 2009	
OCT 2 0 2010	

ANTONINUS' WALL

HADRIAN'S WALL

CHESTER
WROXETER
CAERWENT
SILCHESTER
COLCHESTER
LONDON

LIMES

COLOGNE
MAINZ
SAALBURG
RHEIMS
PARIS
TRIER
SENS
ALÉSIA
ARGENTORATUM

GERMANICU

ARGENTOMAGUS
AUTUN
AUGUSTA RAURICA
CARNUM
AQUI

SAINTES
PÉRIGUEUX
LYONS
BORDEAUX

VIENNA
AOSTA
AQUILEIA
VERONA
POLA
NÎMES
ORANGE
VAISON
SUSA
MONTMAURIN
ARLES
TURBIA
VINTIMIGLIA
SAINT-BERTRAND
GLANUM

CONIMBRIGA
AMPURIAS
ALERIA
ROME
ANCONA
EMERITA
TARRAGONA
ALBA
SAGONTA
OSTIA
PRAENESTE
ITALICA
POMPEII
HERCULANEUM

LIXUS

CHERCHEL
TIPASA
UTICA
CARTHAGE
PIAZZA AR
VOLUBILIS
JEMILA
HIPPONE
LIMES
AFRICANUS
CIRTA THUGGA
(DUGGA)
THUBURBO MAIUS
TIMGAD
LAMBESE
MACTAR
THYSDRUS
SBEITLA
SABRATHA
OEA
LEPTIS MAGN

<u>N.B.</u> This map shows the principal remains extant and does
not necessarily correspond with the great maps of the
Roman world.